Best Wishes from the 16th

Kevin & Debbie Ence
Darrill & Jana Larkin
Dennis & Terry Patton

MARRIAGE
Covenants and Conflicts

MARRIAGE

Covenants and Conflicts

Mark E. Petersen

Bookcraft
Salt Lake City, Utah

Library of Congress Catalog Card Number: 77-81461
ISBN 0-88494-325-9

4th Printing, 1979

Lithographed in the United States of America
PUBLISHERS PRESS
Salt Lake City, Utah

TO
RIGHTEOUS WOMANHOOD

Woman was made from the rib of man.
She was not made from his head, to top him.
Nor from his feet, to be stepped upon.
She was made —
> *From his side, to be equal with him;*
> *From beneath his arm, to be protected by him;*
> *Near his heart, to be loved by him!*

Author Unknown

Contents

Chapter One

Which Way to Go?

John and Karen were at the crossroads. Which way should they go? They had just finished four years of college, but John wanted an advanced degree. The two young people had dated all through their university work and had looked forward to married life together.

And yet they were confused now and quite uncertain about the future. It seemed that so many avenues of activity lay before them, and some looked very promising. But how would their marriage fit in?

They talked about the possibility of getting married now, with Karen "working" John's way through to his degree. They knew of other couples who had done that, but they knew too that some of those marriages had broken up. That frightened them.

If they took that route what would they do about having children? With Karen working and John depending on her pay check, was it practical for her to become a mother? And there was the matter of expenses. Could they afford John's continued schooling and babies too? And would little children disturb John's concentration on his studies?

They talked about postponing the marriage for three years and continuing on a mere dating basis. But there was the possibility that they might drift apart and become interested in other people. Neither wanted that.

There was one alternative they would not choose, however, and that was the worldly one in which two of their friends now lived together without benefit of legal or any other formalities.

As Latter-day Saints these young people had been reared in the traditions of the Church. But they were conscious of the fact that this fast-moving world is rapidly changing its levels of acceptable behavior. Some of their friends had said that the old traditions are no longer tenable—that a new day has dawned, with revised concepts and fewer restraints.

John and Karen were glad that the Church held fast to its moorings and was not shaken by the storm of modernity that swept all about it. They believed firmly that God is unchangeable and that throughout the centuries he has been the same—yesterday, today and forever. He must be. His gospel is constant and its precepts must be the same for all people, regardless of the age in which they live. The Lord is no respecter of persons.

They knew too that over the centuries worldly standards had changed repeatedly, both up and down. It has been said that only one thing is certain, and that is change. And the world does change. But the Lord cannot and will not adjust his eternal rules of right and wrong to fit the caprice of changeable man.

As Latter-day Saints they realized that their point of view must be that of the gospel—the everlasting and never-changing gospel. It would point the direction in which they should go to solve their dilemma.

Chapter Two

The Point of View

There are about 2½ million Latter-day Saints living in the United States. Naturally, like other citizens, they are being bombarded by the philosophies of so-called liberators, both men and women. Members of the Church elsewhere in the world are also subjected to many of the same philosophies. What is to be our attitude?

Latter-day Saint concepts are different from those of the rest of the world, and necessarily so. This is a fact which all Church members should accept. It is what makes us what we are. There is a line of demarcation which we will not cross if we remain loyal to our heritage.

Some compromise their principles and try to live on both sides of the line. But the Lord has told us that we cannot serve God and mammon at the same time. We must be on one side or the other. We are either for him or against him. There is no middle ground. (See Matthew 12:30; Luke 11:23.)

President George Albert Smith used to say: "Stay on the Lord's side of the line. If you cross over the line you are in the devil's territory."

The gospel draws the line. It makes us different from the world—peculiar, possibly, as some say—but rather, and preferably, distinctive. It is something to be proud of.

The gospel of the Lord Jesus Christ provides a way of life in and of itself. It establishes both our standards and our prohibitions. The people of the world do not live it for they know little if anything about it. Hence they establish their own way of life, their own level of satisfaction, and their own methods of achieving happiness.

They seek continued pleasure, excitement and stimulation, but mix in generous amounts of greed and selfishness. This attitude of course is directly opposed to gospel principles and therefore must remain totally unacceptable to Latter-day Saints.

To properly orient ourselves in this confusing world, we must hold strictly to the gospel point of view. As President David O. McKay taught so vigorously, and as is reflected frequently by President N. Eldon Tanner, let us remember who we are and then act accordingly.

And who are we? We are children of God who have made covenants to serve him. Through obedience to those covenants we hope to become like him, or as the Savior said, "Even as I am." (3 Nephi 27:27.)

What portions of the world's teachings that harmonize with gospel teachings we should carefully consider, but what is in opposition to those principles we must shun. Why should we allow worldly thinking to dilute the values we place upon revelation?

It was Paul the Apostle who wrote: "Prove all things; hold fast that which is good. Abstain from all appearance of evil." (1 Thessalonians 5:21-22.)

So it is the gospel which orients us and gives us the correct point of view. It becomes a compass to point our way through the storm, and if followed, it will guide us into the safe harbor.

As we make choices of conduct it will be well to always keep in mind the words of the Savior: "What shall a man give in exchange for his soul?" (Mark 8:37.)

Everything we do has some eternal significance, for each act of our lives leaves an impress upon our character, and it is our character that we take with us into eternity. What shall it be?

Edgar A. Guest wrote:

> The good breeds good and the bad breeds bad,
> We are met by the traits we show. . . .
> Each of us builds the world he knows
> Which only himself can spoil.

In one of her beautiful poems, Elsie Robinson described the courage required to hold our ideals in the face of opposition. She wrote:

> It is not hard to die.
> Any fool can, every fool must
> Die some day.
> But it is extremely hard to live,
> It takes a strong and brave understanding man
> To be willing to live each day
> And not merely exist.
> It takes enormous courage to say
> "I choose to live right—regardless of the cost."

President Calvin Coolidge at one time said:

"What we need is not more material development but more spiritual development; not more intellectual power but more moral power; not more knowledge but more character; not more government but more culture; not more law but more religion; not more of the things that are seen but more of the things that are unseen."

To which Elder Sterling W. Sill added:

"This requires that we stand erect and look up. The beast was thrown down on all fours and thus his vision is cast upon the ground. But man is created upright in the image of his Maker that he might look up to God and to righteousness with his faith in the clouds."

Chapter Three

The Divine Plan

Marriage is ordained of God, and family life is the Lord's program for the development of us, his children. His entire plan of eternal progression is based upon it. Take family life away and we remove every possibility of becoming like our Father in heaven. (See Matthew 5:48.)

The Apostle Paul taught that we are the children, the literal offspring, of God. So he has a family, and we are that family. (See Acts 17:28-29; Hebrews 12:9; Romans 8:16-17.) The whole plan and purpose of our existence is that we become like him. Without this concept our existence would have no purpose or direction.

Could there possibly be any other grand design, any other logical or sensible explanation of our life on earth? Shall we be so blind that we fail to see it and thus lose our great potential? Shall we allow the philosophies of uninspired men to divert us from the truth?

We have a Father in heaven. But can there be a Father without a Mother, and can there be Parents in heaven without the eternal marriage bond which makes the family a family?

President Joseph Fielding Smith wrote: "All men and women are in the similitude of the universal Father and Mother, and are literally sons and daughters of Deity." (Joseph Fielding Smith, *Man: His Origin and Destiny*, Deseret Book Company, 1954, page 351.)

When President Smith discoursed on Genesis and the creation of mankind he quoted: "So God created man in his own image, in the image of God created he him; male and *female* created he them." (Genesis 1:27. Italics added.) Then he said: "Is it not feasible to believe that female spirits were created in the image of a 'Mother in Heaven'?" (Joseph Fielding Smith, *Answers to Gospel Questions*, Vol. 3, Deseret Book Company, 1975, page 144.)

We can hardly forget our beautiful hymn by Eliza R. Snow which says:

> In the heavens are parents single?
> No; the thought makes reason stare!
> Truth is reason, truth eternal
> Tells me I've a mother there.

And then again she wrote:

> When I leave this frail existence,
> When I lay this mortal by,
> Father, Mother, may I meet you
> In your royal courts on high?

We perform marriages in our temples. They always remind us that the purpose of these ceremonies is to preserve our family units for eternity, just as we establish them here on earth. This means a preservation, perpetually, of the father-mother-child relationship within the family circle. It is a divine relationship and is intended to last forever. It is part of exaltation.

But there is still a further and deeper meaning. We are told that the faithful who are eternally married and thus advanced to celestial exaltation will enjoy the privilege of having eternal increase. This promise will really make us like our Father and Mother in heaven. It gives to temple marriage a whole new dimension; it opens up a vast new horizon. We can truly become like God in heaven and can be co-creators with him! (See D&C 131:1-4.)

The Prophet Joseph Smith said this:

"Except a man and his wife enter into an everlasting covenant and be married for eternity, while in this probation, by the power and authority of the Holy Priesthood, they will cease to increase when they die; that is, they will not have any children after the resurrection. But those who are married by the power and authority of the priesthood in this life, and continue without committing the sin against the Holy Ghost, will continue to increase and have children in the celestial glory." (Joseph Fielding Smith, compiler, *Teachings of the Prophet Joseph Smith*, Deseret Book Company, 1938, pages 300-301.)

This doctrine really opens to us a thrilling view of our eternal destiny. It shows in fact that we, as children of God, may truly become like him and do many of the things which he does. It is a staggering thought, but it is a basic doctrine of the gospel. It can be accomplished, however, only through marriage and the family relationship, and that marriage must be solemnized in a holy temple of God here on earth.

In discussing the eternal significance of holy matrimony, President Brigham Young said:

"The whole subject of the marriage relation is not in my reach, nor in any other man's reach on this earth. It is without beginning of days or end of years; it is a hard matter to reach. We can tell some things with regard to it; it lays the foundation for worlds, for angels, and for the Gods; for intelligent beings to be crowned with glory, immortality, and eternal lives. In fact, it is the thread which runs from the beginning to the end of the holy Gospel of Salvation—of the gospel of the Son of God; it is from eternity to eternity." (John A. Widtsoe, compiler, *Discourses of Brigham Young*, Deseret Book Company, 1971 edition, page 195.)

In other words, President Young seems to be saying that we here on earth have not yet grasped the full significance of temple marriage. With this in mind he said further:

"When a man and woman have received their endowments and sealings, and then had children born to them afterwards, those children are legal heirs to the Kingdom and to all its blessings and promises, and they are the only ones that are on this earth.

"There is not a young man in our community who would not be willing to travel from here to England to be married right, if he understood things as they are; there is not a young woman in our community, who loves the Gospel and wishes its blessings, that would be married in any other way; they would live unmarried until they could be married as they should be, if they lived until they were as old as Sarah before she had Isaac born to her." (*Discourses of Brigham Young*, page 195.)

Can we see then how destructive are the man-made teachings which would do away with the family circle, cancel out marriage, and immerse mankind in a "new morality" situation with all its sins and diseases plus the condemnation of God?

Unrepentant adulterers are condemned with those who literally go to hell. Said the Lord about them:

"These all are they who will not be gathered with the saints, to be caught up unto the church of the Firstborn, and received into the cloud. These are they who are liars, and sorcerers, and adulterers, and whoremongers, and whosoever loves and makes a lie. These are they who suffer the wrath of God on earth. These are they who suffer the vengeance of eternal fire. These are they who are cast down to hell and suffer the wrath of Almighty God. . . ." (D&C 76:102-106.)

But those who qualify for exaltation in his presence shall receive "all that my Father hath" said the Savior: "He that receiveth me receiveth my Father; And he that receiveth my Father receiveth my Father's kingdom;

therefore all that my Father hath shall be given unto him." (D&C 84:37-38.)

The Lord enlarges on his description in this manner:

"They are they who are the church of the Firstborn. They are they into whose hands the Father has given all things. They are they who are priests and kings, who have received of his fulness, and of his glory; . . . Wherefore, all things are theirs, . . . And they shall overcome all things." (D&C 76:54-56, 59, 60.)

Can there be a more beautiful concept than this? Is it not worth striving for? Shall we not willingly and anxiously labor to develop this kind of perfection by obeying "every word that proceedeth forth from the mouth of God"? (D&C 84:44.)

This is the essence of our religion. This is what God offers to us in contrast to the teachings of man. And it is all based on true family life, with holy matrimony as its foundation stone.

Chapter Four

Homes in the Making

As like begets like, so good homes provided by faithful parents reoccur in good homes established by their children when they marry. The good tree continues to bear good fruit.

Successful homes begin with sound marriages, and proper marriages begin with selective, wholesome courtship. It is in that dating period that we sow the seeds of our ultimate harvest, whether of joy or of sorrow.

Anciently the Lord decreed that his people should marry within their own faith. This means choosing our close friends from within our own religious circle. It is from among our friends that we find our life's companions.

When the Lord addressed ancient Israel through Moses he told the people that they must not marry unbelievers. In one instance he said: "Thou shalt make no covenant with them, . . . Neither shalt thou make marriages with them; thy daughter thou shalt not give unto his son, nor his daughter shalt thou take unto thy son." (Deuteronomy 7:2-3.)

He then gave his reason: "For they will turn away thy son from following me, that they may serve other gods." (Deuteronomy 7:4.)

When the Lord commanded the Israelites to marry within their own circle, he was very specific in saying: "Let them marry to whom they think best; *only to the family of the tribe of their father* shall they marry." (Numbers 36:6. Italics added.)

He repeated the instruction later and gave as his reason: "Every one of the tribes of the children of Israel shall keep himself to his own inheritance." (Numbers 36:9.)

It was the Apostle Paul who declared to the Saints of his day: "Be not unequally yoked together with unbelievers." (2 Corinthians 6:14.) Again this was to keep the Saints within the faith, and thus provide the unity between husband and wife which is so vital in every good home.

The same instruction has been given by modern prophets. Through all the years of his ministry President Spencer W. Kimball has been close to the youth of the Church and has constantly and wisely advised them.

One of his most persuasive appeals has been directed to the importance of people marrying within their own faith. Like presidents of the Church who have preceded him, he has strongly urged that marriages will be most successful if there is much in common in the background of both parties to the marriage.

He has pointed out that people are happier if they marry within their own race and within their own church. He has urged that Catholics would find most harmony by marrying Catholics, Baptists by marrying Baptists, and similarly with those of other denominations. But especially is this applicable to Latter-day Saints.

At the Stockholm, Sweden, Area Conference in August, 1974, President Kimball said:

"I have warned the youth against the many hazards of interfaith marriages, and with all the power I possess, I have warned young people to avoid the sorrows and disillusionment that comes from marrying out of the Church. Unhappy situations almost invariably result when a believer marries an unbelieving spouse.

"I have pointed out the demands of the Church upon

its members in time, energy and funds; the deepness of the spiritual ties that tighten after marriage and as the family comes; the antagonisms that naturally follow such mismating; and that these and many other reasons argue eloquently for marriage within the Church where husband and wife have common backgrounds, common ideals and standards, common beliefs, hopes and objectives, and above all, where marriage may be eternalized through righteous entry into the holy temples."

Since temple marriage is essential to exaltation in the kingdom of God, every person should plan for it. And that means marrying only within the faith. Nonmembers and inactive members of the Church are not allowed in the temple, only faithful members. If we are to marry in the temple, then we must date Church members who are worthy to enter that sacred place.

When young people begin dating, they cannot tell at first glance whether the individual whom they date is to become their eternal mate. Only continued and careful courtship can determine that.

But from the very beginning they can know whether their dating partner is a member of the Church—and a good member—so that if they become serious, there would be no hurdle to overcome on that point.

Members of the Church should understand the word of God on this subject. In Section 131 of the Doctrine and Covenants the Lord specifically says that temple marriage is a saving ordinance. It is an order of the priesthood. The Lord will give everyone an opportunity to receive it, either here or hereafter.

"In the celestial glory there are three heavens or degrees; And in order to obtain the highest, a man [and a woman] must enter into this order of the priesthood [meaning the new and everlasting covenant of marriage]; And if he does not, he cannot obtain it. He may enter into the other, but that is the end of his kingdom; he cannot have an increase." (D&C 131:1-4.)

That is strong and precise language. It is the law of

God. But it is made even more clear in Section 132 of the Doctrine and Covenants, particularly in verses 15 to 17.

In verse 15 the Lord speaks of those who are satisfied merely with civil marriage and receive no temple sealing. He then explains in verse 16:

"Therefore, when they are out of the world [that is, when they are dead] they neither marry nor are given in marriage; but are appointed angels in heaven, which angels are ministering servants, to minister for those who are worthy of a far more, and an exceeding, and an eternal weight of glory."

In other words, those who do not enter into the new and everlasting covenant of marriage become servants to those who will be exalted. They themselves will not be exalted, not having temple marriages, and not having lived for it.

The Lord then gives this explanation in verse 17: "For these angels did not abide my law; therefore, they cannot be enlarged, but remain separately and singly [unmarried], without exaltation, in their saved condition, to all eternity."

We can see then how vital temple marriage is to our eternal progress. Therefore we should see the importance of both dating and marrying within the faith, having our sacred wedding ceremony performed in the holy temple of God by those possessing the sealing power.

Section 76 of the Doctrine and Covenants also adds light to this matter. When the terrestrial glory is described, so also are those who will go there, and they are those who were not valiant in their service to God during mortal life.

"Wherefore, they are bodies terrestrial, and not bodies celestial, and differ in glory as the moon differs from the sun. These are they *who are not valiant* in the testimony of Jesus; wherefore, they obtain not the crown over the kingdom of our God." (D&C 76:78-79. Italics added.)

How could the Lord speak more plainly? Obviously then our eternal exaltation depends to a considerable extent on the kind of marriage we have. Only a temple marriage will qualify. Our dating habits will determine whether or not it will be a temple marriage. Hence our exaltation in the eternal worlds is directly related to our dating habits.

But with it must be worthiness also, for no unworthy person may enter the temple. And if by some means he does, would the Lord place his approval on an ordinance obtained dishonestly? We may deceive bishops and branch presidents, but never the Lord. Before our sealings are finalized before him, they must be approved by the Holy Spirit of promise. (See D&C 132: 7, 19, 20.)

That puts chastity and integrity where they belong as requirements for exaltation. Some may "fall" in love and lose their virtue, but by proper repentance they may be forgiven. Then if they remain faithful they may still receive their blessings. (See D&C 58:42-43.)

Some misunderstand the Lord on the matter of eternal marriage. There are hundreds of wonderful young women, and some older ones too, who never have an opportunity for a proper marriage and refuse to enter a bad one, knowing that it would be both destructive and degrading. To all such the Lord holds out full hope. Every person who keeps himself or herself clean and faithful will be provided for by the Lord. He will not keep any faithful person out of his kingdom, and if such individuals have not had a proper opportunity for temple marriage in this life, the Lord will provide it subsequently.

Who knows but what a girl's intended mate was struck down in childhood, or died of some disease, or he may have been killed in war and is on the other side waiting for her?

A similar thing may be said for women with unfaithful husbands. If these women will remain faithful to the Lord, he will provide for them. No one can rob us of our salvation. No one else can keep us out of heaven. Only we ourselves can do that. If we keep our covenants with the Lord he will keep his with us and will reward us accordingly.

President Harold B. Lee very wisely said:

"You young women advancing in years who have not yet accepted a proposal of marriage, if you make yourselves worthy and ready to go to the house of the Lord and have faith in this sacred principle, even though the privilege of marriage does not come to you now, the Lord will reward you in due time and no blessing will be denied you. You are not under obligation to accept a proposal from someone unworthy of you for fear you will fail of your blessings.

"Likewise you young men who may lose your lives in a terrible conflict [war] before you have had an opportunity for marriage, the Lord knows the intents of your hearts and in his own time will reward you with opportunities made possible through temple ordinances instituted in the Church for that purpose.

"It is a significant thing to me that the statistics of the Church year after year reveal an almost equal number of males and females. . . . Do you suppose that this is just a coincidence and a fact to be explained by scientific theory, or is it because of an anxious Providence who has ordained it so that all young men and young women who are Church members might find their companions within the Church and through eternal marriage be heirs to the promises of the fulness of his blessings?

"To the end that man and woman might be brought together in this sacred marriage relationship, whereby earthly bodies are prepared as tabernacles for heavenly spirits, the Lord has placed within the breast of every young man and every young woman a desire for association with each other. These are sacred and holy impulses but tremendously powerful.

"Lest life be valued too cheaply or these life processes prostituted to the mere gratification of human passions, God has placed foremost in the category of serious crimes against which we are warned in the Ten Commandments, first, murder, and second only to that, sexual impurity. 'Thou shalt not kill! Thou shalt not commit adultery!'

"Satan in his diabolical cunning would have the girl in her youth by scanty or improper dress or by wanton look fan the flame of passion of her youthful boy companion to unholy bounds and likewise would prompt the lips of the young man to speak suggestive words or obscene tales and to take liberties with his girl companion that encourage the defiling of themselves before God by breaking his divine commandment.

"To the end that youth may not fall into the ways of unwisdom and thus become a prey to evil impulses, the Church counsels you to be modest in your dress and manner and forbid the evil thoughts that would prompt your lips to obscenity and your conduct to be base and unseemly.

"To gain the highest bliss in holy wedlock, the fountains of life must be kept pure. The reward for you who keep yourselves clean and pure and embark upon the sea of matrimony in the Lord's appointed way is to enjoy a love and companionship in home and family that shall last forever." (Harold B. Lee, *Youth and the Church*, Deseret Book Company, 1970, pages 129-130.)

Statistics show that persons who marry out of the Church have only one chance in ten of converting a nonmember spouse. It is true that when there are conversions, happy marriages can result. But when both husband and wife remain in separate churches there can of course be no temple marriage, thus creating an immediate barrier to exaltation. Under these circumstances neither will there be situations where husbands and wives will jointly teach their children and convert them to the true gospel. Often, in order to keep intact a marriage where husbands and wives belong to different churches, they both become totally inactive and attend no church at all.

Statistics reveal some interesting information about people who joined the Church but lapsed into inactivity. Among these individuals 67 percent of all wives had married nonmember husbands, and 42 percent of all the men married nonmember women.

As these figures show, mixed marriages tend strongly toward inactivity in the Church. And inactivity means they are not being valiant in the testimony of Jesus. The scripture says that such individuals will not be allowed in the celestial kingdom, but will go instead to the terrestrial glory where there is no exaltation. (See D&C 76:78-79.)

These same statistics show another interesting fact. Of all the Church inactives above referred to, among the women only 1 percent married in the temple, and only 2½ percent of the men married in the temple.

And what does this mean? That marriage within the faith provides more stable homes and helps to preserve activity in the Church. It shows, therefore, that marriage in the temple is one of our greatest safeguards against both inactivity in the Church and divorce. Divorces of people married in the temple are but a fraction of the ratio for those not married in the temple.

Of course there is no ultimate guarantee that every marriage will succeed. Success depends upon the couple itself and the degree to which they try to make the marriage function. It is necessary to "work" at keeping marriages happy.

One of the most important of all laws with respect to marriage is the Golden Rule: "All things whatsoever ye would that men should do to you, do ye even so to them." (Matthew 7:12.) If every husband and wife did to the other as they would be done by, there would never be any serious conflicts, and selfishness would never create family quarrels with all their continued bitterness.

Complete honesty with each other is all essential. President David O. McKay at one time said: "Never marry a man who would deceive you, who would tell you a lie." And of course deception in a woman is quite as despicable as in a man.

Frequent reading of the Savior's instruction to the Nephites about quarreling is most advisable. Said he:

"There shall be no disputations among you, as there have hitherto been; neither shall there be disputations among you concerning the points of my doctrine, as there have hitherto been.

"For verily, verily, I say unto you, he that hath the spirit of contention is not of me, but is of the devil, who is the father of contention, and he stirreth up the hearts of men to contend with anger, one with another.

"Behold, this is not my doctrine, to stir up the hearts of men with anger, one against another; but this is my doctrine, that such things should be done away." (3 Nephi 11:28-30.)

When we quarrel, therefore, we do so by the spirit of the devil, and that spirit is destructive of all that is good, even in family relationships. It is the Spirit of God which is the spirit of love, harmony and peace, which is so essential in making a marriage succeed.

Chapter Five

The Revealed Law

T he exalted view of marriage as held by this Church is given expressly in five words found in the 49th section of the Doctrine and Covenants, 'Marriage is ordained of God.' "

So spoke President David O. McKay as he discoursed on that important subject. How different from the uninspired teachings of men, so many of whom seek to destroy marriage and the home!

President McKay continued: "That revelation was given in 1831 when Joseph Smith was only twenty-five years of age. . . . It is your duty and mine to uphold the lofty conception of marriage as given in this revelation and to guard against encroaching dangers that threaten to lower the standard of the ideal home."

He then added: "Truly no higher ideal regarding marriage can be cherished by young people than to look upon it as a divine institution. . . . The sacredness of the marriage covenant is dangerously threatened. There are too many thoughtless, hasty marriages entered into without enough time taken to consider the temporal or eternal consequences. . . .

"America seems to be drifting toward a low level as regards the law of family and home, with the result that sin and crime are increasing to an alarming extent among the youth of our fair land. I mention these things not in the spirit of pessimism nor as a crier of impending calamity, but with the desire to call attention to the necessity of our maintaining the high standard of marriage set forth in the revelations of the Lord." (*Gospel Ideals*, Improvement Era, 1953, pages 462-463.)

It is of major interest to note that President McKay spoke those words more than forty years ago. He was a prophet of God. Through the eye of revelation he perceived what was coming, and now—today—we see a fulfillment of his words.

How can we, who uphold our prophets, turn our backs upon words like that? This was prophecy given in 1935. We see the results of the worldly attack on the institution of the home even more so now. It is all about us. We should be properly warned and forewarned against such encroachments. Although living in the world, there is no need for us to partake of its Babylon-like sins.

President McKay gave six points on which our people may plan a happy marriage:

First, their relationship must be based on purity.

Second, their religious views must be the same.

Third, their vows should be made with the idea of preserving an eternal, unbroken union, not to be destroyed by petty misunderstandings or difficulties.

Fourth, they need to understand that the covenant made in God's presence in the temple and sealed by the holy priesthood is more binding than any other bond.

Fifth, they must realize that marriage thus commenced is as eternal as love, the most divine attribute of the human soul.

Sixth, they must plan for a family unit that shall remain unbroken throughout eternity.

President McKay also spoke of the responsibility married couples must assume to have children and rear families in the faith. He said:

"Some young couples enter into marriage and pro- crastinate the bringing of children into their homes. They are running a great risk. Marriage is for the purpose of rearing a family, and youth is the time to do it. I admire these young mothers with four or five children around them now, still young, happy."

At another time he wrote:

"The Lord has told us that: '. . . whoso forbiddeth to marry is not ordained of God, for marriage is ordained of God unto man. Wherefore, it is lawful that he should have one wife, and they twain shall be one flesh, and all this that the earth might answer the end of its creation.' (D&C 49:15-16.)"

President McKay then continued:

"By direct revelation, in this passage we have stated in a few words, the purpose of marriage. It is to bear children and rear a family. Let us keep that in mind. Hundreds are now saying, and hundreds more will say—'How can I marry and support a bride in a manner with which she has been accustomed? How can I get an education and support a family?...'

"These are practical questions, and our boys and girls are facing them. I am willing to recognize these and other difficulties and meet them, keeping in mind what the Lord has said that 'marriage is ordained of God for man.' And I repeat that the very purpose of marriage is to rear a family and not for the mere gratification of man or woman. Keeping this thought uppermost in married life, we shall have fewer difficulties and more readily find content."

With this in mind he further said:

"Love realizes his sweetest happiness and his most divine consummation in the home where the coming of children is not restricted, where they are made most welcome, and where the duties of parenthood are accepted as a co-partnership with the eternal Creator.

"In all this, however, the mother's health should be guarded. In the realm of wifehood, the woman should reign supreme." President McKay continued: "The marriage covenant does not give the man the right to enslave her or abuse her or to use her merely for the gratification of his passion." (*Gospel Ideals*, pages 466-467, 469, 471.)

President Spencer W. Kimball spoke on this matter at the Stockholm, Sweden, Area Conference of the Church in August, 1974:

"After marriage young wives should be occupied in bearing and rearing children. I know of no scriptures or authorities which authorize young wives to delay their families or to go to work to put their husbands through college. Young married couples can make their way and reach their educational heights, if they are determined."

He quoted President J. Reuben Clark, Jr. from a general priesthood conference session in October 1949 as follows:

"There is some belief, too much I fear, that sex desire is planted in us solely for the pleasures of full gratification; that the begetting of children is only an unfortunate incident. The direct opposite is the fact. Sex desire was planted in us in order to be sure that bodies would be begotten to house the spirits; the pleasures of gratification of the desire is an incident, not the primary purpose of the desire.

"As to sex in marriage, the necessary treatise on that for Latter-day Saints can be written in two sentences: Remember the prime purpose of sex desire is to beget children. Sex gratification must be had at that hazard. You husbands: be kind and considerate of your wives. They are not your property; they are not mere conveniences; they are your partners for time and eternity."

President Kimball then continued:

"As we talk about marriage, we remember, as Luke says: 'Strive to enter in at the strait gate: for many, I say unto you, will seek to enter in, and shall not be able.' (Luke 13:24.)

"Only through celestial marriage can one find the straight way, the narrow path. Eternal life cannot be had in any other way. The Lord was very specific and very definite in the matter of marriage. He said: 'For this is a day of warning, and not a day of many words. For I, the Lord, am not to be mocked in the last days.' (D&C 63:58.)

"And so we wonder why, with all these blessings and promises, that people will fail to marry correctly and thus waste their lives in a frozen wilderness that may never thaw. Why will any young person ever give a single thought to a marriage out of the temple and jeopardize those glories that are available? Why would a person with a temple marriage think of divorce, of breaking up a family, or of immoralities and infidelities? Why, oh why?" (Spencer W. Kimball, "The Marriage Decision," *The Ensign*, February 1975, pages 4-6.)

Chapter Six

Why We Have Temples

The gospel is a religion of faith and works, and also of covenants. We are the Lord's covenant people, and therefore covenants hold a major place in our religion.

The Jews are spoken of as the covenant race, and they are truly one of the covenant peoples of the Lord. But so are we. Like the Jews we are descendants of Abraham, Isaac and Jacob. The Jews are descendants through Judah, but we are through Joseph. By birth, therefore, we are as much the covenant people of the Lord as are the Jews.

But we are even more so, for we make personal covenants with the Lord through our activities in the Church. These covenants begin with baptism. They are included in ordination to the holy priesthood; they are vital in the sacrament of the Lord's Supper and are found also in the ordinances of the holy temples.

All the covenants are similar—that we agree to serve the Lord with all our hearts and "live by every word that proceedeth forth from the mouth of God." (D&C 84:44.) In return, if we are faithful he will bless us with his Holy Spirit in this life, and in the life to come "all that my Father hath" will be ours. (D&C 84:38.)

The covenants are related directly to the ordinances of the gospel. (See D&C 20:37, 77, 79.) Some of these ordinances may be administered anywhere, as long as they are done properly and by divine authority. For example, we may baptize in a stream, in a lake, in the ocean, or in a font inside a chapel. Likewise, we may confirm new members as is convenient. We administer the sacrament of the Lord's Supper under many different circumstances. Men may be ordained to the priesthood in a chapel or in any other place properly authorized.

But there are some ordinances which the Lord reserves for performance only in dedicated temples. These ordinances pertain to the further blessings of the holy priesthood and include the endowment, marriages, sealings, and baptisms for the dead. (See D&C 95:8; 105:33; 121:19; 124:29-39; 128:1-18.)

All of the ordinances of the gospel, whether performed in or out of a temple, are essential to our exaltation in the kingdom of heaven. Many have supposed that temple ordinances, and particularly temple marriages, were optional. Some have even thought that marriage in a temple was but a fad. But it was never so.

Temple ordinances are as essential for exaltation as is baptism. Temple marriage itself is as much a saving ordinance as is baptism. We can no more be exalted in the kingdom of heaven without our endowments and a temple marriage than we could without baptism in water for the remission of sins.

Joseph Smith was asked at one time if all of these ordinances are necessary, and he replied: "Any person who is exalted to the highest mansion has to abide a celestial law, and the whole law too." (*Teachings of the Prophet Joseph Smith*, page 331.)

The gospel ordinances are for admission into the celestial kingdom. No ordinances are required for admittance to the lower areas, for such areas are provided for the disobedient.

President Brigham Young spoke of the importance of

the endowment in this way:

"The commandments . . . with regard to the ordinances of the house of God are obligatory upon us. Every individual who is prepared for the celestial kingdom must go through the same things. It is absolutely necessary that the Saints should receive the further ordinances of the house of God before this short existence shall come to a close, that they may be prepared and fully able to pass all the sentinels leading into the celestial kingdom and into the presence of God.

"Then go on and build temples of the Lord, that you may receive the endowments in store for you, and possess the keys of the eternal Priesthood, . . . and be made acquainted with the laws of angels, and of the kingdom of our Father and our God, and know how to . . . enter fully into the joy of your Lord." (*Discourses of Brigham Young,* pages 395-396.)

Sealing ordinances are performed in the temple. What are they? By sealing we mean that a man and his wife, under the authority of the priesthood, are bound, or wedded, to each other forever. Children who are born after parents have been sealed in the temple are automatically sealed or bound to their parents and no additional ordinance of sealing is required. These children are spoken of as having been born under the covenant. But if they are not born under the covenant they may be sealed to their parents in the temple.

The sealing ordinance is very important. Anciently Jesus gave to the apostles the power that whatsoever they should bind on earth should be bound in heaven, and whatsoever they loosed on earth should be loosed in heaven. (See Matthew 16:19; 18:18.)

That same authority was given to our modern prophets. (See D&C 127:7; 128:8.) It is by that authority that all the temple ordinances are performed.

The Lord said to the Prophet Joseph Smith:

"For I have conferred upon you the keys and power of the priesthood, wherein I restore all things, and make known unto you all things in due time.

"And verily, verily, I say unto you, that whatsoever you seal on earth shall be sealed in heaven; and whatsoever you bind on earth, in my name and by my word, saith the Lord, it shall be eternally bound in the heavens; and whosoever sins you remit on earth shall be remitted eternally in the heavens; and whosoever sins you retain on earth shall be retained in heaven.

"And again, verily I say, whomsoever you bless I will bless, and whomsoever you curse I will curse, saith the Lord; for I, the Lord, am thy God." (D&C 132:45-47.)

When Hyrum Smith, the brother of the Prophet, was appointed to be the patriarch to the Church, succeeding his father in that position, the Lord instructed: "Whatsoever he shall bind on earth shall be bound in heaven; and whatsoever he shall loose on earth shall be loosed in heaven." (D&C 124:93.) Hence Hyrum was given the sealing power.

Who restored the keys of sealing in these last days? Elijah the prophet came to the Kirtland Temple on April 3, 1836. Of the keys he restored, the Prophet Joseph Smith wrote: "The spirit, power, and calling of Elijah is, that ye have power to hold the key of the revelations, ordinances, oracles, powers and endowments of the fulness of the Melchizedek Priesthood and of the kingdom of God on the earth; and to receive, obtain, and perform all the ordinances belonging to the kingdom of God, even unto the turning of the hearts of the fathers unto the children, and the hearts of the children unto the fathers, even those who are in heaven."

The Prophet further added: "Then what you seal on earth, by the keys of Elijah, is sealed in heaven." And then he said by way of command: "The first thing you do, go and seal on earth your sons and daughters unto yourself, and yourself unto your fathers in eternal glory." (*Teachings of the Prophet Joseph Smith*, pages 337, 338, 340.)

He also said: "The Saints have not too much time to save and redeem their dead, and gather together their living relatives, that they may be saved also, before the earth will be smitten, and the consumption decreed falls upon the world. I would advise all the Saints to go with their might and gather together all their living relatives to this place, that they may be sealed and saved, that they may be prepared against the day that the destroying angel goes forth." (*Teachings of the Prophet Joseph Smith*, page 330.)

The Prophet Joseph Smith spoke of the endowment in this language: "If a man gets a fulness of the priesthood of God he has to get it in the same way that Jesus Christ obtained it, and that was by keeping all the commandments and obeying all the ordinances of the house of the Lord." (*Teachings of the Prophet Joseph Smith*, page 308.)

It is obvious then what great importance the Prophet Joseph placed upon the temple ordinances. There was great urgency during his day to have the early temples of the Church built and dedicated because the Lord had promised that therein he would reveal these important ordinances to the modern Saints. (See D&C 124:37-42.)

The Lord said that his people are always commanded to build temples unto his holy name. (See D&C 124:39.) And why? So that these saving ordinances may be given us, for without them we can never receive our exaltation.

Some people have wondered why the Saints continued to build the Nauvoo Temple after the Prophet was martyred and when the mobs were on the verge of driving the Saints out of the city. The Saints carried on, building at times with a trowel in one hand and a gun in the other for protection against the mobs. And why? Because their salvation depended on it.

One of the first things Brigham Young did when he arrived in Salt Lake Valley in 1847 was to designate the place where the Salt Lake Temple was to be constructed. And why? Because the Saints needed those sacred ordinances, available only in a temple, for without them they could not receive their exaltation.

It was the same with the St. George Temple, the Manti

Temple and the Logan Temple. Our hardy pioneers built those temples so that they could obtain their higher ordinances.

Our people of today must realize the urgency and importance of this subject, even as did the pioneers. Our salvation cannot be complete without the temples. Then why do we not take temple ordinances more seriously?

Who, knowing the facts, would accept a civil marriage if a temple marriage could be obtained? Temple marriage is the only one to which God gives eternal significance. It is his mode of marriage, just as immersion is his mode of baptism.

The Lord does not accept sprinkling or pouring as valid modes of baptism. Only immersion is acceptable; it alone is the divine symbol of the burial and resurrection of the Savior.

The Lord tolerates civil marriage during mortality, but in a civil marriage death becomes a divorce court which severs the marriage bonds upon the demise of one or the other of the parties involved. As persons enter into a civil marriage they then and there agree that it will be dissolved when death comes to either party. It is inherent in the ceremony.

As immersion is God's mode of baptism, so temple marriage is his one and only form of marriage in the eternal sense. To reject God's mode of baptism is to reject membership in his true Church and a remission of sins. To reject temple marriage is to reject fellowship and progress in the highest degree of glory in the world to come. It prevents us from achieving the ultimate goal—that of becoming perfect even as our Father in heaven is perfect.

As President Kimball expressed it: "Why, oh why, cannot people see it? Why do so many fail to seek its great blessing?"

In the temples we have special rooms where sealings take place. They are adjacent to the celestial room. Each temple also has a veil. When Jesus was crucified the veil in the temple at Jerusalem was rent in twain.

The veils of our modern temples open into the celestial room. It is through these veils that the Saints pass in order to enter the celestial room. This act is symbolic of our passing through the eternal veil from mortality into immortality and, if we are worthy, also into celestial glory.

The celestial rooms of the temples are the most beautiful rooms in those holy edifices. And yet, the sealing rooms adjacent to them are fully in keeping with the celestial rooms in appearance and furnishings. They are also beautiful. It is there that celestial marriages are performed. No other place is so appropriate for a marriage. No other place has such an atmosphere, such a spirit of purity and peace.

Within these sealing rooms a couple may kneel at the altar of God, clasp hands symbolic of an eternal union, and receive the blessing of the holy priesthood whereby they are sealed or bound together as man and wife for time and all eternity, and may have their children sealed to them for eternity as well. There is nothing to compare with it anywhere in the world.

So much to be desired was this blessing of eternal marriage that the pioneers risked their lives and donated even the widow's mite to construct these sacred buildings. Likewise, Saints today sacrifice to build temples, whether in Europe, South America, the Orient, North America or the South Seas. It is all the same. The spirit never varies, the sense of willingness to sacrifice is ever present as Saints realize the vital importance of temples in their lives.

Understanding all this, how could anyone be satisfied with worldly matrimony? How could some even consider rejecting marriage altogether? Proper marriage is truly the gateway to exaltation, and so important is it in the eyes of the Lord that he has provided his holy temples in which these ceremonies may be performed.

There is probably no other instance wherein the contrast between worldliness and godliness is so pronounced. When it is recalled that some young couples marry in so-called "wedding chapels" with a worldly atmosphere, others marry in the office of a mayor or a justice of the peace, and still others reject the ceremony altogether, it is heartbreaking that they would not choose the beauty and the purity of the Lord's way in the temple in preference to anything else.

But who can contrast godliness and worldliness? They are as far apart as the poles.

Chapter Seven

Heaven on Earth

A happy home is not only heaven on earth but it is the strength of the nation. A people, a nation, cannot be great without happy, strong homes."

Speaking in the Tangerine Bowl meeting in Orlando, Florida, December 18, 1976, President Spencer W. Kimball, with those strong words, made an eloquent appeal to the nation for the preservation of its homes.

He is not the only one who has compared good home life to heaven on earth. Others of our leaders have done so, but likewise have the many thousands of Latter-day Saints who, by their righteous living, actually enjoy that kind of life here and now.

In our beautiful hymn "Love at Home," we have these words:

> There is beauty all around
> When there's love at home;
> There is joy in every sound
> When there's love at home.
> Peace and plenty here abide,
> Smiling sweet on every side.

Time doth softly, sweetly glide
When there's love at home.

In the cottage there is joy
When there's love at home;
Hate and envy ne'er annoy
When there's love at home.
Roses bloom beneath our feet;
All the earth's a garden sweet,
Making life a bliss complete
When there's love at home.

Kindly heaven smiles above
When there's love at home;
All the world is filled with love
When there's love at home.
Sweeter sings the brooklet by;
Brighter beams the azure sky;
Oh, there's One who smiles on high
When there's love at home.

President David O. McKay voiced these same feelings when he said:

"I know that a home in which unity, mutual helpfulness, and love abide is just a bit of heaven on earth. I surmise that nearly all of you can testify to the sweetness of life in homes in which these virtues predominate. Most gratefully and humbly, I cherish the remembrance that never once as a lad in the home of my youth did I see one instance of discord between Father and Mother and that good will and mutual understanding have been the uniting bond that has held together a fortunate group of brothers and sisters. Unity, harmony, good will are virtues to be fostered and cherished in every home." (*Gospel Ideals*, pages 477-478.)

A "heavenly" home here on earth must be created and maintained. It was President Joseph F. Smith who said:

"A home is not a home in the eye of the gospel, unless there dwell perfect confidence and love between the husband and the wife. Home is a place of order, love, union, rest, confidence, and absolute trust; where the breath of suspicion of infidelity can not enter; where the woman and the man each has implicit confidence in each other's honor and virtue." (Joseph F. Smith, *Gospel Doctrine*, Deseret Book Company, 1966, page 302.)

Elder ElRay L. Christiansen said: "No nation is better than its homes. The Church, the School, and even the Nation stand helpless before a weakened and degraded home in building the character of children. If our nation is to endure, the home must be safeguarded, strengthened, and restored to its rightful and important place." (Emerson Roy West, compiler, *Vital Quotations*, Bookcraft, 1968, pages 160-161.)

Elder Richard L. Evans said: "All things need watching, working at, caring for, and marriage is no exception. Marriage is not something to be indifferently treated or abused, or something that simply takes care of itself. Nothing neglected will remain as it was or is, or will fail to deteriorate. All things need attention, care and concern, and especially so in this most sensitive of all relationships of life." (Richard L. Evans, compiler, *Richard Evans' Quote Book*, Publishers Press, 1971, page 16.)

Most scholars say that it is not marriage that fails, it is people that fail.

President Abraham Lincoln understood this principle, and before entering his marriage he said: "Whatever woman may cast her lot with mine, should any ever do so, it is my intention to do all in my power to make her happy and contented; and there is nothing I can imagine that would make me more unhappy than to fail in that effort." (*Richard Evans' Quote Book*, page 19.)

But how do we work at obtaining such a happy marriage?

President Kimball, in an address to Brigham Young University students, September 7, 1976, gave this advice:

"Love is like a flower, and, like the body, it needs constant feeding. The mortal body would soon be emaciated and die if there were not frequent feedings. The tender flower would wither and die without food and water. And so love, also, cannot be expected to last forever unless it is continually fed with portions of love, the manifestation of esteem and admiration, the expressions of gratitude, and the consideration of unselfishness. . . .

"To be really happy in marriage, one must have a continued faithful observance of the commandments of the Lord. No one, single or married, was ever sublimely happy unless he was righteous. There are temporary satisfactions and camouflaged situations for the moment, but permanent, total happiness can come only through cleanliness and worthiness. . . .

"Two individuals approaching the marriage altar must realize that to attain the happy marriage which they hope for, they must know that marriage is not a legal coverall; but it means sacrifice, sharing, and even a reduction of some personal liberties. It means long, hard economizing. It means children who bring with them financial burdens, service burdens, care and worry burdens; but also it means the deepest and sweetest emotions of all. . . .

"There must be a great unselfishness, forgetting self and directing all of the family life and all pertaining thereunto to the good of the family, subjugating self. There must be continued courting and expressions of affection, kindness, and consideration to keep love alive and growing. There must be a complete living of the commandments of the Lord as defined in the gospel of Jesus Christ.

"With these ingredients properly mixed and continually kept functioning, it is quite impossible for unhappiness to come, misunderstandings to continue, or breaks to occur. . . . Marriage never was easy. It may never be. It brings with it sacrifices, sharing, and a demand for great selflessness."

Many teachings of the scriptures are applicable to marriage. Basic to all is the commandment to love the Lord with all our heart, mind, might and soul. In marriage, that law means bringing the gospel into the home so that its influence may guide all that is done there.

The second commandment to love our neighbor as ourselves is very appropriate indeed for marriage. Who are our closest neighbors? Those of our own family! And we are to love them at least as well as we love ourselves. In other words, there is no place for selfishness in the home.

The Lord gave us the commandment to do to others as we would be done by. This Golden Rule implements the second great commandment as nothing else can. Serve others. Eliminate selfishness. Treat others in the way we would like to be treated. This will bring love and joy to every home.

Judging and criticizing others in the home is one of the worst of the heartbreakers. The Lord commanded that we should not judge each other. What should we do instead? We should treat the other as we would like to be treated; turn the other cheek; forgive trespasses; be helpful and kind instead of critical.

One of the great formulas for Latter-day Saint living appears in the Doctrine and Covenants: "Remember faith, virtue, knowledge, temperance, patience, brotherly kindness, godliness, charity, humility, diligence." (D&C 4:6.)

Bring these into a marriage, and will it ever fail? They are among the great laws of heaven. Transferred into the home, will they not make it heavenly also?

But both partners in the marriage must work to bring this condition about. One alone is left powerless in this respect.

Chapter Eight

The Wise Virgins

Jesus likened the kingdom of heaven unto ten virgins "which took their lamps, and went forth to meet the bridegroom. And five of them were wise and five were foolish.

"They that were foolish took their lamps, and took no oil with them: But the wise took oil in their vessels with their lamps.

"While the bridegroom tarried, they all slumbered and slept. And at midnight there was a cry made, Behold, the bridegroom cometh; go ye out to meet him.

"Then all those virgins arose, and trimmed their lamps. And the foolish said unto the wise, Give us of your oil; for our lamps are gone out. But the wise answered, saying, Not so; lest there be not enough for us and you: but go ye rather to them that sell, and buy for yourselves.

"And while they went to buy, the bridegroom came; and they that were ready went in with him to the marriage: and the door was shut.

"Afterward came also the other virgins, saying, Lord, Lord, open to us. But he answered and said, Verily I say unto you, I know you not. Watch therefore, for ye know neither the day nor the hour wherein the Son of man cometh." (Matthew 25:1-13.)

This parable is significant for several reasons. The one most often mentioned is the advice to be ever ready for the Lord's coming, for no one knows when it shall be.

But there is tremendous importance also to the fact that a wedding theme forms the basis of this lesson in which the Savior is designated as the Bridegroom.

Going with the Lord into his eternal kingdom is likened to entering with him into this wedding feast. It was a well-chosen simile. Without proper marriage there is no exaltation in his kingdom, and those who fail to make the right preparation through the sealings of the temple jeopardize their eternal status, even as did the virgins who had no oil in their lamps.

It is of more than ordinary interest that reference to the Savior as the Bridegroom, with marriage as a central theme, recurs repeatedly in the scripture, thus emphasizing its eternal significance.

When John the Baptist was asked by the Jews if he were the Messiah, he replied:

"I am not the Christ, but that I am sent before him. He that hath the bride is the bridegroom: but the friend of the bridegroom, which standeth and heareth him, rejoiceth greatly because of the bridegroom's voice: this my joy therefore is fulfilled. He must increase, but I must decrease." (John 3:28-30.)

In the Book of Revelation we read:

"Let us be glad and rejoice, and give honor to him: for the marriage of the Lamb is come, and his wife hath made herself ready. . . . Blessed are they which are called unto the marriage supper of the Lamb." (Revelation 19:7, 9.)

In a slightly different setting the marriage of the bride and her husband is further mentioned: "And I John saw the holy city, new Jerusalem, coming down from God out of heaven, prepared as a bride adorned for her husband. . . . Come hither, I will shew thee the bride, the Lamb's wife." (Revelation 21:2, 9.)

And in modern revelation we read: "Wherefore, be faithful, praying always, having your lamps trimmed and burning, and oil with you, that you may be ready at the coming of the Bridegroom." (D&C 33:17.)

Again: "Yea, a voice crying, Prepare ye the way of the Lord, prepare ye the supper of the Lamb, make ready for the Bridegroom." (D&C 65:3.)

And then this: "Prepare ye, prepare ye, O inhabitants of the earth; for the judgment of our God is come. Behold, and lo, the Bridegroom cometh; go ye out to meet him." (D&C 88:92.)

"Yea, let the cry go forth among all people: Awake and arise, and go forth to meet the Bridegroom; behold and lo, the Bridegroom cometh; go ye out to meet him. Prepare yourselves for the great day of the Lord." (D&C 133:10.) The warning is also given elsewhere in scripture.

But why this repeated reference to the married state with Jesus as the Bridegroom? The Lord obviously is attempting to fix in our minds the supreme importance of proper marriage for all who enter his kingdom.

He spoke also of the protection of the home against evil intruders, for example, and said:

"Know this, that if the goodman of the house had known in what watch the thief would come, he would have watched, and would not have suffered his house to be broken up." (Matthew 24:43.)

Usually we think of this scripture in reference to a thief entering the home to steal some of the good man's property. But when he speaks of the home being "broken up," could he have had in mind a worse offense than the break in of an ordinary thief—an intruder who would vandalize but not actually "break up" a home? Could he have meant also the possible dissolution of the family circle because some covetous person imposed infidelity upon that home and thus broke it up?

The Lord also spoke of his "household," and asked: "Who then is a faithful and wise servant, whom his lord hath made ruler over his household?" (Matthew 24:45.)

The Lord's "household" is a vital part of his kingdom. Is it not the foundation of stable living in mortality and the basis of progress in eternity?

When he labored among the Nephites his teachings again were family-oriented. He called the people together as families, he blessed their children, and he taught family prayer: "Pray in your families unto the Father, always in my name, that your wives and your children may be blessed." (3 Nephi 18:21.)

Is it any wonder that the marriage theme is so basic in his gospel? Exaltation comes only to those who have been married in the temple and remain faithful. We can become like our Father in heaven, but only if we have these blessings.

The temptations of the world should not blind us to our eternal opportunities. Their arguments and their procedures are but the foolishness of men when compared to the wisdom of God.

Here again we may see the necessity of staying on the Lord's side of the line.

Chapter Nine

Limited Families

In the year 1910 the general population of the United States reached a total of 92,000,000. During that year, the mothers of the land gave birth to 2,777,000 babies.

In 1976, with a population of nearly 250,000,000, American mothers gave birth to only 3,128,000 children. How the ratio has dropped!

More babies were born in 1961 than in any other year in the history of the nation. The total for that year was 4,268,000. In 1976 American mothers gave birth to 1,140,000 fewer babies than they did in 1961.

This decline of course is a direct result of numerous abortions and the free use of the "pill" and other forms of contraception. The frightful tragedy of the wholesale destruction of unborn children is appalling to right-thinking people.

The attitude of the leaders of the Church toward curtailing families has been forcefully expressed over and over again for years. Certain types of birth control were a threat even in the days of President Brigham Young. It was he who said:

"There are multitudes of pure and holy spirits waiting to take tabernacles, now what is our duty? To prepare tabernacles for them; to take a course that will not tend to drive those spirits into the families of the wicked, where they will be trained in wickedness, debauchery, and every species of crime. It is the duty of every righteous man and woman to prepare tabernacles for all the spirits they can." (*Discourses of Brigham Young*, page 197.)

President Joseph F. Smith said:

"I regret, I think it is a crying evil, that there should exist a sentiment or feeling among any members of the Church to curtail the birth of their children. I think that is a crime wherever it occurs, where husband and wife are in possession of health and vigor and are free from impurities that would be entailed upon their posterity. I believe that where people undertake to curtail or prevent the birth of their children that they are going to reap disappointment by and by. I have no hesitancy in saying that I believe this is one of the greatest crimes of the world today." (*Gospel Doctrine*, pages 278-279.)

President David O. McKay spoke as follows:

"Any effort or desire on the part of a married couple to shirk the responsibility of parenthood reflects a condition of mind antagonistic to the best interests of the home, the state and the nation. No doubt there are some worldly people who honestly limit the number of children and the family to two or three because of insufficient means to clothe and educate a large family as parents would desire to do, but in nearly all such cases the two or three children are no better provided for than two or three times that number would be.

"Such parents may be sincere, even if misguided; but in most cases the desire not to have children has its birth in vanity, passion, and selfishness. Such feelings are the seeds sown in early married life that produce a harvest of discord, suspicion, estrangement and divorce.

"All such efforts often tend to put the marriage relationship on a level with the panderer and the courtesan. They befoul the pure fountains of life with the slime of indulgence and sensuality. Such misguided couples are ever seeking but never finding the reality for which the heart is yearning." (*Gospel Ideals*, page 468.)

Although the brethren teach us that the purpose of marriage is to "multiply and replenish the earth," at no time have they taught us to go to extremes. It is not required that a woman should have a child every year. Some might be able to do so and maintain their health, but a great many women cannot. Common sense should prevail, as President McKay has said.

The health of the wife is vital. There certainly is no point in her having children so frequently that she dies in the process, leaving her little ones to be reared by other people. Husbands should love their wives enough to avoid excesses of all kinds and realize that there is great wisdom and strength in self-control.

Some women may have physical limitations which prohibit a normal birth, and there is a limit to the number of Caesarean sections one may have. Others develop kidney and related complications which force a limitation of children. Some women simply cannot carry children and have repeated miscarriages, while still others cannot become pregnant at all. Many have called in the elders to administer to them, seeking a healing from these conditions.

Women in casual conversation, not knowing about such intimate facts, certainly should not criticize their neighbors who may dearly want to have more children if they could. Who is to judge another anyway? Some women with only one or two children may have tried conscientiously to have more, but still were not able to do so.

On the other hand, some women avoid childbearing by resorting to abortions. This subject as we know it today, reached extensive proportions subsequent to President McKay's day. In order to meet it now the First Presidency has issued the following statement:

"The Church opposes abortion and counsels its members not to submit to, be a party to, or perform an abortion except in the rare cases where, in the opinion of competent medical counsel, the life or health of the woman is seriously endangered or where the pregnancy was caused by forcible rape and produces serious emotional trauma in the victim. Even then it should be done only after counseling with the local bishop or branch president and after receiving divine confirmation through prayer.

"Abortion is one of the most revolting and sinful practices in this day, when we are witnessing the frightening evidence of permissiveness leading to sexual immorality.

"Members of the Church guilty of being parties to the sin of abortion are subject to the disciplinary action of the councils of the Church as circumstances warrant. In dealing with this serious matter, it would be well to keep in mind the word of the Lord stated in the 59th Section of the Doctrine and Covenants, verse 6, 'Thou shalt not steal; neither commit adultery, nor kill, nor do anything like unto it.'

"As far as has been revealed, the sin of abortion is one for which a person may repent and gain forgiveness." (*The Ensign*, July 1976, page 76.)

Chapter Ten

We Will Not Starve!

Shall we refuse to marry or, if we do marry, shall we limit our families in the fear of growing people faster than we grow food? The idea is ridiculous, many experts now say.

A *Time Magazine* essay on the population explosion estimated that the farmers of the world could feed a population forty times as large as the present number on earth if they worked up to their potential.

Two points are made clear by this and other articles: First, that there is still much space left on earth, and second, that we can produce all the food we now need or will need in the foreseeable future if we will but do so.

In the September 13, 1971, issue of *Time Magazine* appeared this interesting article:

"Parts of the world—the slums of great cities like New York, London and Tokyo—are obviously overcrowded. But this does not mean that the entire planet is running out of room. Although India has a major population problem, with about 570 million people crammed into 1.1 million square miles, Australia has more than twice that much land and only 1/40 the population. Canada, Brazil and Russia all have vast empty spaces. And although much of this space is jungle or steppe or desert, the Israelis have demonstrated in the Negev that technology and hard work can make the most inhospitable land support new settlers.

"Obviously, international migrations are not a likely prospect, but even within any one nation, crowding is generally a result of the drift from rural areas to the city. Taken as a whole, the U.S. still has only 58 people per square mile—scarcely one-sixth the density of Switzerland, which does not seem terribly crowded. But about 70% of all Americans have jammed together onto 2% of the land, while half of the nation's counties lost population during the past decade. . . .

"Experts suggest that America's optimum population is still to be attained. Professor Donald J. Bogue, director of the University of Chicago's Community and Family Study Center, speculates that the U.S. population can be 'twice what it is now without much difficulty,' and that there will be even less difficulty if 'the cities of this country can be greatly decentralized.' Ben Wattenberg, a demography expert and former White House staffer, adds: 'There is no optimum population as such. Whether we have 250 million people or 350 million people is less important than what the people, however many of them there are, decide to do about their problems.' "

It is of more than passing interest that experts who have studied the problem of feeding the underprivileged nations have come to the conclusion that their food shortage is not caused by the inability to produce food so much as by the political systems in some countries that prevent their national development to a point where they can feed themselves.

A free nation, such as America, has had the liberty to develop its technology. Technology has produced more food. But in nations where such freedom does not exist, such technology is not available and advancement does not come.

R. J. Rushdoony, writing "The Myth of Over-Population" for the University Series Historical Studies (Craig Press, Nutley, New Jersey), goes so far as to say: "The answer then to our problem is in essence this: socialism always creates ultimately an imbalance between the number of people living and their food supply which results in hunger or famine. There is in this sense therefore always a problem of over-population under socialism. Hunger is chronic and endemic to socialism." And less than a third of the world lives under free governments.

The United States has done a great deal to teach other nations better agricultural techniques, and with marvelous results. For example, Mexico for many years produced only 500 pounds of wheat per acre, but it now grows 2,300 pounds. Ten years ago the Philippine Islands imported a million tons of rice each year. Now they are self-sustaining and looking for export markets. West Pakistan has increased its wheat production by 171 percent and its rice yield by 162 percent. Sadly, however, as much as 20 percent of its crop is lost to rodents, thieves and foreign smugglers.

One of the great lessons people should learn in this life is that God knows what he is doing.

Since we are told repeatedly by certain groups that we are growing people faster than we are growing food and that worldwide famine may strike, we should remember that the Lord is governing the universe and that he does all things well.

Among other things the Lord controls the number of people coming to earth, and in his creation he provided that if we will do our part, none need go hungry, and certainly none need starve.

He said in one of his revelations to the Prophet Joseph Smith: "For the earth is full, and there is enough and to spare." (D&C 104:17.)

He said this as he was talking about care of the poor. He went on to refer to the "abundance which I have made" and then outlined his policies regarding the handling of property. He would not have mentioned his "abundance" if it were not there; neither would he have said there is "enough and to spare" if the contrary were true.

Scientists who have carefully studied the world food situation are frank to say that one of the main reasons for shortages is the black market in certain underprivileged countries; others speak of the dreadful waste in those lands.

An organization known as The Continental Group, made up of a number of large corporations representing interests in various nations, reports: "Food production has outpaced population growth for the past twenty years; and food growth is progressing more rapidly in developing nations."

As reported in *Newsweek* magazine, waste is the greatest cause of hunger, not underproduction. It was said that 1,200 million tons of cereal are produced each year, 360 million tons of which go to waste.

The comment reads: "If just this amount was distributed to the 460 million malnourished people in the world, each would have 1,500 pounds of grain, the same amount consumed by people in developed nations."

The report also indicated that food spoilage in the United States is only 15 percent compared to 50 percent in India.

Agricultural experts have pointed out that much waste in underdeveloped nations is due to poor distribution methods and a great lack of warehousing, causing tons of American food to be piled on foreign docks or on the ground, and thus wasted away in backward lands.

The earth will feed all the spirits the Lord has assigned here if only mankind will use some degree of wisdom. But as the Lord says, "I . . . have given unto the children of men to be agents unto themselves." (D&C 104:17.)

So if food runs short, let us not blame the Lord.

Chapter Eleven

The "Singles Trend"

Worldly efforts to break down the family concept have had a tragic effect on some people, it is true, but in the overall, the family is still triumphant.

Morton Hunt, writing in the *Family Circle* magazine under the title "Why Open Marriage Failed," commented on the predictions of sociologists that infidelity would cause family life to come to an end. He says:

"What has happened in the five to ten years since these predictions were the talk of the town? Almost nothing.

"The predictions have simply not come true. There is no evidence that American marriages are becoming sexually open. In fact, the great majority of American women still consider fidelity by their husbands—and themselves—extremely important. They still view infidelity by either spouse as profound disloyalty."

He then cited results of nation-wide surveys to sustain his conclusion. One of these surveys indicated that nine-tenths of all persons contacted insist on complete fidelity in marriage.

He quoted one writer as saying that our cultural history, our traditions, our way of bringing up children to believe in complete fidelity and virtue "are powerful enduring forces."

There is a vicious ground swell of immorality and infidelity to be sure, but the basic fabric of America is holding firmly to family unity, with, in most cases, mutual devotion on the part of most husbands and wives toward each other.

There are some unfortunate trends, of course. One of them is the drift of many single people—divorced, widowed or never married—to resort to a separate way of life.

In the January 31, 1977, issue of *U.S. News & World Report* appeared a study of the subject, and it begins with this paragraph:

"An emerging life style centered around the activities of the unmarried men and women is adding a new dimension to American cities and towns. The 'singles phenomenon' is affecting housing, social contracts, and recreation on a scale America has never seen before."

The article indicated that a third of all households in the United States are now headed by "singles," either widowed, or divorced, or by persons who never have married.

On February 8, 1977, the *Deseret News* carried a UPI story out of Washington which said:

"An emerging social trend of the 1970s is the escalating number of men and women living together out of wedlock, the Census Bureau says.

"The number of unmarried couples in the United States who have decided to share living quarters has more than doubled since 1970.

"Arthur Norton, who directed preparation of the study, said the phenomenon is not a passing fad. 'This is a true, accepted social trend,' he said, adding that he expected the number of unmarried roommates to increase even more.

"The report said that in March 1976, when the statistics were compiled, 1,320,000 unmarried Americans lived with a member of the opposite sex in a two-person household, compared with 654,000 in 1970.

"Forty-eight percent of the men and 43 percent of the women involved had never been married, the report said."

In some cities "singles" have concentrated in certain housing areas where the well-to-do pay anywhere from four hundred dollars for a one-bedroom apartment to as much as twenty-five hundred dollars per month for sumptuous penthouse accommodations. On the other hand, there are the "singles of the slums" who outnumber the well-to-do and who live in rooming houses that are far beneath a desirable standard. One California rental complex reports having more units let to unmarried people than to married couples.

There are of course the millions of "singles" who are solid, substantial, and respectable citizens, many of whom would marry if the proper opportunity came along. There are also thousands of crippled or otherwise handicapped individuals who are in no position to marry and yet live wholesome lives.

And there are hosts of young people working in all walks of life who seem to be victims of circumstances in this aggressive world of ours. They are a decided asset to any community. Although included in the overall statistics they are less vocal and pose no problems and hence are seldom heard from.

Taken altogether the unmarried portion of the population is no where near sufficient to change the balance which now is so far in the favor of the married couples. And in any case, the majority of these single people are good citizens, and they alone will out-balance the undesirable element among the unmarried.

Through Church and other agencies, many of these good young people, and a fair number of older ones who are widows, widowers or divorcees, are finding mates and marrying, even though it comes later in life than they had originally hoped for.

The whole picture with the unmarried population is a fluctuating one, and poses no threat to the nation. The institution of home and family is so well entrenched in America and so generally recognized as the basic strength of the nation, that no extremist may take comfort from limited trends among singles which they may wish to balloon all out of proportion in their calculations.

Chapter Twelve

Consider the Unforeseen

Although it is important for young women to look toward marriage and to prepare for it, it would also be wise for them to consider the possibility that they may not marry at all in this probation or marry later in life.

In any event, they should get an education and find a skill or a career that will be challenging and stimulating to them. By so doing they will be in a position to provide for themselves while seeking a proper companion.

Unfortunately, many girls do not look beyond their high school or college days. Their interest lies solely in finishing their schooling and getting married. They fail to realize that they may not marry as soon as they desire, nor do they consider what they will do in the interim.

In their search for happiness and contentment, they feel that marriage is the only answer. When they do not marry until later, they become restless and do not find rewarding or challenging occupations.

They would do well to plan and prepare for a profession or a career that would be enjoyable and interesting to them. This preparation would also be helpful if for some unforeseen reason they were put in a position of supporting themselves and a family later on in life.

Many girls who do not keep this in mind find themselves wandering through life, going from job to job and from city to city seeking contentment and a purpose. They feel that although they may be discontented and unhappy while single, marriage will be the panacea for all. They fail to realize that happiness comes from within and each one must make her own happiness, whether married or single.

Such individuals should bear in mind what Samuel Johnson has said:

"The fountain of content must spring up in the mind. He who has so little knowledge of human nature as to seek happiness by changing anything but his own disposition, will waste his life in fruitless efforts and multiply the griefs he purposes to remove."

Many girls make the tragic mistake of marrying for the wrong reason. Because of social or other pressures they will enter into almost any marriage simply to be married.

In one case a young lady was anxious to be married following her mission. She was in her mid-twenties and felt she must marry before turning thirty years of age. She met a man some years her senior who had been married and divorced. He had six children, the oldest being only a few years younger than herself. After only a three-week courtship they were married, outside of the temple. She now has three children of her own and has had continuous problems both with his children and his former wife. She has learned the hard way that there are things much worse than being single.

She was unable to find happiness for herself while single and has been just as unsuccessful in trying to make herself and her family happy following her marriage. As a result, she has now turned to the ways of the world in her struggle through life.

In many instances girls who have not looked into the future and have not planned for a possible alternative, for a stimulating and fulfilling occupation in the interim, find themselves untrained and doing work which they do not particularly enjoy. By the time they realize they may not marry in this life they feel it is too late to get proper training in a field that would be meaningful and interesting to them. They discover that too many years have passed. Because of financial limitations and other ramifications they are unable to obtain the desired education to enter a more challenging and rewarding field, and thus they feel unqualified to make a worthwhile contribution to society.

Individuals who find themselves in the position of being single would be benefitted by keeping in mind the words of President Harold B. Lee when he said:

"Some of you do not now have a companion in your home. Some of you . . . may not yet have found a companion. In your ranks are some of the noblest members of the Church—faithful, valiant, striving to live the Lord's commandments, to help build the kingdom on earth, and to serve your fellowmen.

"Life holds so much for you. Take strength in meeting your challenges. There are so many ways to find fulfillment, in serving those who are dear to you, in doing well the tasks that are before you in your employment or in your home. The Church offers so much opportunity for you to help souls, beginning with your own, to find the joy of eternal life.

"Do not let self-pity or despair beckon you from the course you know is right. Turn your thoughts to helping others. To you the words of the Master have special meaning: 'He that findeth his life shall lose it: and he that loseth his life for my sake shall find it.' (Matthew 10:39.)

"Also appropriate are the words of King Benjamin: 'And behold, I tell you these things that ye may learn wisdom; that ye may learn that when ye are in the service of your fellow beings ye are only in the service of your God.' (Mosiah 2:17.)" (Harold B. Lee, from the film *Strengthening the Home,* 1973.)

Chapter Thirteen

What the Facts Show

A̶ll that glitters is not gold.

The magazine *Saturday Review* reported on a book written by George Gilder. The title of the work is *Naked Nomads: Unmarried Men in America*. The book says that unmarried men are the most desperate and unhappy people in our society. Earl Nightingale, broadcasting in his "Our Changing World," also quoted from this book, and he said that unmarried men are most likely to turn to criminality, to suicide, or to be institutionalized. Statistically, they make half the money that married men do, and far less than single women. They also age more rapidly than do married men, the book reported.

Sixty percent of all criminals are single. In this connection author Gilder says that we should blame the single state rather than poverty as being the major factor in the commission of crime. He says singleness rather than race is the most significant factor in the incidence of poverty and crime among blacks.

Mr. Gilder acknowledges of course that there are exceptions in many cases. He knows that public opinion seems to picture the bachelor as "the swinging, carefree, happy character with plenty of money and lots of girls to choose from." But he says the facts are just the opposite. The least happy person in our society is the bachelor.

The fruits of the no-restraints concept are already beginning to surface among the looser element of our society. The national epidemic of venereal disease is one of those frightful fruits. More than five thousand new cases are reported daily, not to mention probably at least as many more that go unreported. The majority of these cases occur among people ranging from fifteen to twenty-five years of age, most of whom are single.

Crime reports must include the increased lawlessness involving "liberated" women. *Time Magazine* for December 1, 1975, reported:

"Though American women are much less confined to the home these days, liberation does not always lead to useful pursuits. FBI statistics released last week indicate a record 18% jump in crimes in 1974, and women were involved in more of them than ever before. In the past 15 years, robberies committed by women have risen 306%, larcenies (mainly shoplifting) 404%, frauds and embezzlements 332%, and forgeries and counterfeiting 167%.

"Women are committing mostly petty offenses—only one in six homicides is attributed to a woman—but criminologists expect them to work their way up (or down) the ladder. Sociologist Francis Ianni of Columbia University believes this trend is the 'criminal analogue' of the women's liberation movement. As in business, politics and education, there will be equal opportunities in crime. You can't have Bella Abzugs without Bonnie Parkers."

Juvenile crime related to one-parent families is alarming. In one western state 45.6 percent of all juvenile delinquents come from one-parent homes.

Chapter Fourteen

The Working Wives

In 1976, according to U.S. Department of Labor reports, another million American housewives entered the labor market. This brings the total of working women to 39,719,000 in the nation, of whom 25,800,000 are wives or mothers.

It is estimated that within five years, if the trend continues at the present rate, 42 percent of all husband-wife households will be included in that category. At present 48 percent of all American women and girls over sixteen go out to work.

In some cases, wives work from sheer necessity. Many husbands cannot find jobs either because they are unskilled, beyond the desirable hiring age, or ill. Many women whose families are grown and gone find useful employment.

But millions of younger married women just want to get out of the home. They are encouraged to do so by the women's liberation people whose program seeks to "emancipate" mothers from the home and "lift their sights to higher and better things."

They don't stop to count the cost. Instead they seem to

regard the home as a place of confinement, housework as a drudgery, and tending little children as an encumbrance, not to mention the task of rearing them.

Singularly enough, they and others are now demanding that social security be provided for wives based on a fair-wage scale. They forget that such a tax would add notably to the expense of running a home. More especially, the plan would downgrade the wife to the position of a paid housekeeper and take from her the glory that crowns true motherhood.

But here child neglect enters the picture. Social workers have found little ones locked up in homes for a full day at a time by mothers who had left them alone and went out to work. Other children have been found locked out of their homes after school and left on the streets for hours, waiting for mothers to come home from work.

A good many young working wives accept shift jobs and take their turn working nights. Many a marriage has been undermined during "coffee breaks" and other rest periods, or during the night hours after work, as a result of clandestine courtships originating there. In numerous cases where both husband and wife work, the husband takes one shift and the wife another. They are like ships that pass in the night.

What kind of family life can be achieved under such conditions? And what is the effect upon the children who in large measure are robbed of the intimate care of both father and mother, and who never come to know what a proper family circle is really like?

It is interesting indeed that some 50 percent of all juvenile delinquency cases come from homes where both father and mother reside, but where, for the most part, parents fail to create a proper home environment in which to train their children. This exceeds even the 45 percent of all delinquency cases which come from one-parent homes. It is no wonder that social workers and juvenile court officers lay most of the child delinquency blame on the doorstep of the home.

Nearly all runaways leave homes of that kind, most of them resenting deeply the lack of direction given by parents to their own offspring. Much of the child abuse comes in these circumstances too, particularly the sexual abuse of young daughters in the home. It is no wonder they run away from homes such as that.

President Kimball, in a general conference address, discussed these matters. He quoted first from *Parents Magazine* regarding working wives as follows:

"Most of the married women over 35 in the labor force are working not because their families really 'need the money,' but in order to maintain a higher standard of living, get away from some housework, and lead, as they suppose, a more interesting and richer life."

He then went on:

"A prominent judge listed the causes of juvenile delinquency:

"First, destructive toys and games such as guns and other symbols of violence. Second, working mothers; and third, fathers who work two shifts, absenting themselves from the home except to eat and sleep.

"His long list of causes ended with this: Lack of religious training and discipline in the home and schools, and lack of love in the home. My reference is Judge Jacob M. Braude of the Circuit Court of Cook County (Chicago), Illinois.

"These lacks were inherent in the parents, but it was the children who suffered.

"In the labor force are about 2.5 million women whose children are under six, and 5.4 million with children under twelve years of age. Think of it: a possible twelve to fifteen million children without a mother through crucial hours! Of these about 400,000 children under twelve years of age must care for themselves entirely while their mothers work.

"One-third of all mothers with children under eighteen are in paid employment. My statistics come from the Children's Bureau of the U.S. Department of Health,

Education and Welfare and other dependable sources. This means that in this country, one child in 13 under 12 must look out for himself. In the 10-11 year old group, the ratio is one in five without care while the mother is at work."

Chapter Fifteen

Working Fathers

Much is said about working mothers, and especially those who allow their outside interests to bring about a serious neglect of home and family. But what about the fathers who do the same thing, or worse?

Some fathers allow business to rule their lives. They let it rule out of their lives the precious home ties that in reality should be most important to them.

Some allow recreation to do the same thing. While there are many who take their families on vacation trips, there are also many who choose their cronies in preference to their families and go on fishing or hunting trips with "adult only" groups and give little thought to the needs of their loved ones.

And then there are those who allow social activities to so fill up their lives that again the families are crowded out.

Even some Church workers are guilty of family neglect. Some of these brethren, in addition to being busy with their daily employment, also have certain social responsibilities or political appointments, and still attempt to carry on a full-scale program of Church assignments as well. The net result is that the family is given too little thought and even less attention. Is that the purpose of married life?

One father was called to the police station where his son was being held with other boys on a robbery charge. As he talked with the officers he said that he could not understand how his son ever got into this kind of trouble. The boy was well housed in one of the finest neighborhoods; he had his own car and was given plenty of spending money. What excuse was there for a robbery? the father wondered.

The police sergeant asked if the father had ever heard of boys playing pranks because they had little else to occupy their time. The father admitted that he had, but thought his boy would never be guilty of such a thing.

The officer then asked the father how much time he spent each day or week or month in training his son in character-building pursuits. As the father looked back over the days and weeks, he remembered that he had seldom sat down with his son for a father-son conversation. He hadn't taken him fishing or hunting in several years, nor did they ever work together, even in the yard. Since the father didn't have time for church-going, the son followed in his footsteps and never went to church either.

With little if any restraint at home, the young man sought friends outside, and they were the street crowd. First they indulged in vandalism, then in petty thievery, and now they were arrested for armed robbery. Who was most to blame, the father or the son?

Having a family is more than procreation, and it is more than paying the family bills. Having a family requires *rearing* of the children, and that requires time, attention, patience, understanding, and a desire to make of the child a good citizen, an honorable member of the family, and a solid member of the Church.

Every father needs to budget his time as carefully as he does his money, and a fair part of the allotment of time should go to the family. Of course he must attend to his employment, that goes without saying, and he certainly must give a certain proportion of time to the Church, but he should be "temperate in all things."

President David O. McKay said at one time: "The father, who because of business or political or social responsibilities, fails to share with his wife the responsibilities of rearing his sons and daughters, is untrue to his marital obligations, is a negative element in what might be and should be a joyous home atmosphere, and is a possible contributor to discord and delinquency." (*Gospel Ideals*, page 477.)

Men and women marry for companionship. They should continue to provide it throughout their lives. They also marry to have families, which is commanded of the Lord. The family responsibility is to be mutually shared between husband and wife.

One of the most important things about good family life should be religion, and the gospel of the Lord Jesus Christ should be made the pivot about which the entire program of fathers, mothers and children should move. Without the gospel no family life can be truly successful. With it, if it is brought into the home and practiced there by all concerned, family life need never fail.

One of the basic rules of success in marriage is the Golden Rule, to do to others as we would be done by. That rule applies to husbands and wives by all means; but also it relates to fatherhood and motherhood, the *rearing* of the children, which must include the teaching of our young people by precept and example, and providing wholesome companionship for them.

Every boy is bigger and better if he has a good father who makes a companion of him. Every girl is likewise better if she has a father she can be proud of, who takes the leadership of the home in wholesome pursuits, and who establishes in the minds of the girls what good manhood is. This then becomes a criterion for their selection of boys they may sometime want to marry. And every wife is a better wife if her husband is an honorable man.

Fathers should budget certain evenings of every week when they will be home with their families. Busy men like bishops should plan for free evenings home with the family as well as all day Saturdays for family outings, family work activities, or other "do it together" projects.

Sunday evenings should be family evenings, and Monday night should always be reserved for home evening. Where could we find a better opportunity than in the home evening for the development of filial happiness, mutual understanding, and the creation of faith in the hearts of children? Home evening is one of the greatest blessings to come into the lives of Latter-day Saints.

One of the chief causes of juvenile delinquency today is the failure of parents to teach their children the value of work. Every child should have certain assigned chores. Each should learn a skill of some kind. Farm families are fortunate in having plenty of work for growing children to do, but city families must sometimes create work opportunities for their children. Work is one of the greatest blessings of God to man, and unfortunate indeed is the boy or girl who never learns to love it.

As Latter-day Saints it is our responsibility to convert our children to the restored gospel of the Lord Jesus Christ. The father holds the priesthood and presides in the home—in righteousness. He is not to be domineering, cruel, or unkind in any way. He should be a Christian gentleman who loves the Lord and is therefore Christlike in his attitudes.

As the presiding one in the family, it is his responsibility to see that gospel principles and standards are upheld in the home and that children are converted to the gospel and learn to love it.

Fathers and mothers are expected to act in complete harmony in these matters. In a spirit of true partnership they are to so operate conditions in their homes that their children will learn to be upright, honest, true Latter-day Saints.

Missions should always be kept in mind for the boys,

who should have this ideal held before them from their early childhood. Savings accounts for missions should be started as soon as the boys are old enough to understand. Each one should have it as his personal goal that he will fill a mission and that he will prepare in childhood for that great service.

To both boys and girls alike temple marriage should be taught, with a clear understanding that it is one of the cherished goals in life. But all of this must come from the parents; no father can leave it alone to his wife, and no wife should attempt to leave it alone to her husband. Both must cooperate to achieve these purposes. President McKay said, out of our homes come the future leaders of the government as well as of the Church.

The President then said: "Let us cherish in our homes as we cherish the lives of our children themselves that word *honor* with all the synonyms—respect, reverence, veneration; honoring mother, honoring father, having them honor us as we honor and revere God our Eternal Father. Let the element of honor, devotion, reverence permeate the home." (*Gospel Ideals*, pages 483-484.)

Prayer should be a vital part of each home, with family prayers being said each night and morning and with all members of the family being taught to daily say their individual private prayers.

How better could we conclude this chapter than to again quote President McKay: "Our country's greatest resource is our children. Next to eternal life, the most precious gift that our Father in heaven can bestow upon man is his children." (*Gospel Ideals*, page 487.) Then dare we neglect them?

Chapter Sixteen

The Young and Abandoned

Teenage marriages are constantly increasing. Many of them are traced to improper family conditions. There are thousands of young daughters who thoroughly dislike their own homes and who seek some degree of security in marriages of their own. Hence they marry even though still too young.

One of the very sad facts in these instances, however, is that statistics show that of all the girls who marry while in their teens, 70 percent were pregnant before the marriage took place. In one western state 44.4 percent of all resident brides of all ages had married as teenagers.

It is among such young people that divorce figures reach their highest point. And it is no wonder. On what basis could those young people hope to build a happy marriage? Most of them never knew what good family life was like. They learned only from the bad examples of their own parents. They knew nothing better.

Some of these young mothers remarry later in life, but many of these divorced girls are left with the responsibility of rearing the children born to them from these undesirable marriages. Government statistics indicate that there are over seven million children under fourteen years of age being raised in homes where there is no father present.

A new point of view with respect to teenage pregnancies is being mentioned by some psychologists. They claim that many young girls simply want to be mothers and are not particularly attracted to the mere excitement of sex. They have what the psychologists call the "baby doll syndrome." They want a little baby to play with as they formerly played with dolls. When the infant grows to the point where it seems to become a "person," the young mother tires of it and wants to get pregnant again and have still another "baby doll." The validity of this supposition may be open to question, but sociologists dealing with these girls say that this is a new and recurring factor.

Then there are the thousands of mothers who are abandoned by husbands who go astray and deliberately avoid all financial and moral responsibility for their families. Marvelous are the mothers in these circumstances who shoulder full responsibility for their families, who supply sustenance for them, and who provide the love and care of a true mother.

Many of these devoted but abandoned women teach their children the gospel, uphold honesty and integrity, send their boys on missions, labor in their wards, hold regular family prayers, conduct home evenings, and otherwise rise to every requirement of Latter-day Saints with respect to their families. Surely they deserve a crown of glory for what they do. Their children honor them for the sacrifices they make. Some great men and women have come from such homes, powerful evidence of the value of good family influence.

Certainly not all mothers neglect their children even if they work, nor do all nonworking mothers provide ideal homes. Some women who are not employed spend more time away from home with civic and social clubs or church-related activities than do a good many others with full-time jobs. There are those who stay home all of the time but alienate their families with negative attitudes and hence are a bad influence.

The really important question is, How much time and what quality of time does she devote to her family? Is her family neglected because of her social or other outside activities, even though she does not work? Does she make her husband and children feel important and wanted? Does she take pleasure in performing those tasks which make a house a home? Does she place a proper value on her "mothering" responsibilities in the home?

Does she take time to give each member of the family a sense of self-importance and confidence, a feeling of security and contentment? Does she really follow the teachings of Christ in relation to the other members of the home? Does her kind and cheerful attitude and her warmth reach out to each individual in the home?

If she does her part in the family circle, whether she goes to work or not, usually she will be rewarded with great personal happiness and a true sense of accomplishment. And the real compensation will be in that her children will most likely live productive and happy lives.

But no woman can be successful in building a good home—and neither can any man—without the divine influence of the gospel of the Lord Jesus Christ. Worldly influences must not be allowed to thwart the purposes of the Lord, nor the intentions of his people to serve him. Worldliness exacts its price, and the price of godlessness is beyond the ability of anyone to afford.

Elder Albert E. Bowen of the Council of the Twelve once wrote:

"You can't destroy in a people reverence for and a proper submission to the highest authority ever recognized by man—the Supreme Being—without setting in action the sapping forces which must ultimately destroy reverence for and a willingness to submit to all lesser authorities. With faith in God gone, you cannot hold faith in mortals. With divine law repudiated you can't perpetuate acceptance of human law nor hold allegiance to it.

"When morality, in the sense of those things that entail permanent personal and social consequences, wholly departs from any system, that system destroys itself by its own greed and vileness. Indulgence in excess weakens the whole organism; it fosters lusts and usurpations and hates. That the 'wages of sin is death' is as sure as the judgments of God."

Chapter Seventeen

What TV Has Done

Television is a mixed blessing, as everyone knows. Whereas some of the best of our culture appears on its screen, certainly much of our worst is repeatedly displayed and absorbed by our youngsters, some of whom spend as much as forty to fifty hours per week watching it.

In the February 1977 issue of the *Education Digest* appeared an article entitled "The Disturbing Changes in the American Family." It indicates that many parents have abdicated to television the responsibility of tending their children. It says that "by the time the average American youngster graduates from high school he has spent more hours watching television than in any other activity except sleeping."

"And," it says, "we are paying the price for this growing inattention, even hostility, to our children. Accidents among children appear to be increasing, child abuse by parents has become a national problem. Nor should all the blame fall on the parents themselves. It is not only the parents of children who are neglecting them, society does so too. And in many ways the crux of the problem is not the battered child but the battered parent who exists in a society exerting pressures which may undermine the role of the parents and the functions of parenthood.''

Then it makes this daring statement:

"What has replaced the parents, relatives, neighbors, and other caring adults? Three things primarily: television, peer groups (same-age cliques or gangs), and loneliness. Today, children at all age levels show greater dependency on their age-mates than they did 10 years ago. And increasing numbers of lonely 'latch-key children' are growing up with almost no care at all, often running away to join colonies of other solitary juveniles and to experiment with drugs, crime, sex, religious cults, and the sheer restless busy-ness of Kerouac-like movement over the American landscape. These children contribute more than their proportion to the ranks of young persons who have reading problems, are dropouts, use drugs, and become juvenile delinquents.

"What is not often recognized is that the tearing of the social fabric which so many people feel around them is largely a result of deteriorating family life and declining care for our children.''

Newsweek Magazine also published an article on this same subject in February 1977. It said:

"The wonder of it all is that the worry about television has so belatedly moved anyone to action. After all, the suspicion that TV is turning children's minds and their psyches toward mayhem is almost as old as the medium itself.

"But it is only in recent years that social scientists, child psychologists, pediatricians and educators have begun serious study of the impact of television on the young.

" 'The American public has been pre-occupied with governing our children's schooling,' says Stanford University psychologist Alberta Siegel. 'We have been astonishingly unconcerned about the medium that reaches into our homes. Yet we may expect television to alter our social arrangements just as profoundly as printing has done over the past five centuries.' "

The magazine then quotes Dr. Benjamin Bloom of the University of Chicago to the effect that by the time a child reaches five years of age, he has undergone as much intellectual growth as will occur over the subsequent thirteen years. And yet, the magazine says, children under five watch TV an average of 23.5 hours per week.

Newsweek then says:

"The conclusion is inescapable: after parents, television perhaps has the most influence on the beliefs, attitudes, values and behavior of those who are being raised in its all-pervasive glow."

Then the news magazine says:

"The overwhelming body of evidence—drawn from more than 2,300 studies and reports—is decidedly negative. Most of the studies have dealt with the antisocial legacy of video violence. Michael Rothenberg, a child psychiatrist at the University of Washington, has reviewed 25 years of hard data on the subject—the 50 most comprehensive studies involving 10,000 children from every possible background. Most showed that viewing violence tends to produce aggressive behavior among the young. The time is long past due for a major, organized cry of protest from the medical profession in relation to what, in political terms, is a national scandal, concludes Rothenberg.

"An unexpected salvo was sounded when the normally cautious American Medical Association announced that it had asked ten major corporations to review their policies about sponsoring excessively gory shows. 'TV violence is both a mental-health problem and an environmental issue,' explained Dr. Richard E. Palmer, president of the AMA. 'TV has been quick to raise questions of social responsibility with industries which pollute the air. In my opinion, television . . . may be creating a more serious problem than air pollution.'

"Reaction was immediate: General Motors, Sears Roebuck and the Joseph Schlitz Brewing Co. quickly announced they would look more closely into the content of the shows they sponsor.

"The AMA action comes in the wake of a grass-roots campaign mobilized by the national Parent-Teacher Association. The 6.6 million-member PTA recently began a series of regional forums to arouse public indignation over TV carnage. If that crusade fails, the PTA is considering organizing station-license challenges and national boycotts of products advertised on offending programs."

Temple University conducted an in-depth study of the subject, the results of which were reported by UPI in a New York dispatch:

"For millions of American children, the shadow of fear is a constant companion, and it looms largest for those whose daily routine includes a heavy dose of television, a Temple University survey indicated Tuesday.

"The survey, conducted by Temple's institute for Survey Research under sponsorship of the Foundation for Child Development, revealed two-thirds of the 2,200 children interviewed expressed fear that 'somebody bad' might get into their homes.

"A fourth of the children said they were afraid someone would hurt them if they went outside to play, and more than half said they were afraid when their parents argued.

"Researchers conducting the survey said the number of children sampled represented a scientific cross-section of 17.7 million boys and girls, aged 7 to 11.

"Dr. Orville G. Brim, president of the foundation, said the survey found the highest level of fear in children who watch television for four hours or more on weekdays, and he recommended federal action to protect young viewers from the negative effect.

"More than half the children said they are allowed to watch television any time they wish to. More than a third are allowed to watch any program they choose."

Motion picture producers, in an effort to help the public sort out the good from the bad among the movies shown in theaters, have suggested a rating index of PG (parental guidance) for some of their films. Although this is not totally effective, it might give a hint to parents with respect to the TV programs they allow their children to see.

Few parents will go to a theater to preview a PG-rated film to determine whether their children should see it. But every parent in the home is able to see enough of a picture along with the child to determine whether it is suitable. And certainly parents can note the advance advertising provided by TV for many features. This advanced publicity usually reveals the character of the film. Even some of these previews, however, are shocking beyond anything a child should see.

Parental guidance is the key to this problem, but to provide the guidance the parents must be on the ground—in the home—where the action takes place.

Chapter Eighteen

Dating Trends

Some dating looks toward marriage which is clean and honorable. Other dating looks toward temporary physical excitement and occasionally to relationships without benefit of marriage or any other formal arrangement; and the consequences are tragic.

Many parents feel frustrated over the dating habits of their rebellious young people who seem to throw wisdom and good judgment to the winds and turn their backs upon all their training, both in the home and in the Church.

Dating of this kind usually is the result of infatuation. Youth so involved seem to ignore every sound and honest principle. They are rebellious, and parents often are nearly helpless. Advice is the last thing such young folks want. In their eyes, parents have outlived their usefulness and have become obstacles to their self-expression and happiness. Such youth resent even a small suggestion concerning their behavior. When the matter reaches that point, little can be done. The rebellion must soften first.

But parents must always try. It does no good to force rebellious young people, for this they strongly resist. Love is the answer, even though parents must repeatedly turn the other cheek. There comes a time when love will be remembered and, when least expected, it may bear the desired fruits.

Of course the safest course parents can take is to train their children from infancy in acquiring righteous standards, choosing proper friends, and teaching them to love wholesome things. Usually this bears the fruit we want. Generally the words of Solomon are right when he said that if we train up a child in the way he should go, when he is old he will not depart from it. Usually this is true. Some of our best-trained young people are tempted and fall, however. But this is the exception.

When the exception appears, it of course breaks our hearts. We must patiently endeavor to love our dear ones back again. Some times this never happens, but often it does. By and large, good training pays off. Strong families generally remain strong families, even though there may be an occasional black sheep.

Without training, failure is almost a certainty. But there are exceptions there too, for some good young people come from homes of careless parents but were influenced by good friends.

Training in chastity, of course, is one of our greatest safeguards, especially when it is given in the light of the gospel of Christ and when it is seen in proper perspective with the whole plan of the Lord.

It has been said that the best defense is a strong offense, and if our righteous offense is well prepared and builds good character, it becomes the most effective defense we can have against the evils of the world.

President David O. McKay said:

"The highest ideal for our young girls today, is love as it may be expressed in marriage and home building, and this virtue in which love finds true expression is based upon the spiritual and not the physical side of our being. If marriage and home building be based upon physical attraction alone, love will sooner or later become famished and home life a heavy, disheartening existence." (*Gospel Ideals*, page 449.)

President McKay also said:

"The dominant evil of the world today is unchastity. I repeat what appeared over the signature of President Joseph F. Smith while he was living:

" 'No more loathsome cancer disfigures the body and soul of society today than the frightful affliction of sexual sin. It vitiates the very fountains of life and bequeaths its foul effects to the yet unborn as a legacy of death.'

"The question is: What have you made of yourself— your character?

"He who is unchaste in young manhood is untrue to a trust given him by the parents of the girl, and she who is unchaste in maidenhood is untrue to her future husband and lays the foundation in the home of unhappiness, suspicion, and discord.

"Do not worry about these teachers who say something about inhibitions. Just keep in mind this eternal truth, that chastity is a virtue to be prized as one of life's noblest achievements. It contributes to the virility of manhood. It is the crowning virtue of womanhood, and every red-blooded man knows that is true. It is a chief contributing factor to a happy home; it is the source of strength and perpetuity of the nation." (*Gospel Ideals*, page 399.)

President Brigham Young taught in his day:

"Any man who humbles a daughter of Eve to rob her of her virtue and cast her off dishonored and defiled, is her destroyer, and is responsible to God for the deed. If the refined Christian society of this century will tolerate such a crime, God will not; but he will call the perpetrator to an account. He will be damned; in hell he will lift up his eyes, being in torment, until he has paid the uttermost farthing and made full atonement for his sins.

"The defiler of the innocent is the one who should be branded with infamy and cast out from respectable society, and shunned as a pest, or, as a contagious disease, is shunned. . . . His sin is one of the blackest in the calendar of crime, and he should be cast down from the high pinnacle of respectability and consideration, to find his place among the worst of felons."

President Young then added:

"The man who abuses, or tries to bring dishonor upon the female sex is a fool, and does not know that his mother and his sisters were women." (*Discourses of Brigham Young*, page 194.)

President Harold B. Lee very thoughtfully said:

"I would impress upon you that despite changed conditions and the abnormal times during which you have lived and are now living, the standards of right and wrong have not changed, but are as eternal and as unchanging as the stars in the heavens.

"The youth of all generations have faced tests just as severe as those you are facing. Their strength to overcome great odds came from an abiding faith in themselves and faith in the ultimate triumph of truth. The same powers and influences that guided your parents through their youthful days are with us today and will be efficacious in your behalf to just the extent that you heed the counsel of the Church and live as the gospel teaches." (*Youth and the Church*, pages 15-16.)

When young people fall before temptations they must always remember the Lord's kindly invitation to repentance and reformation of life, as will be discussed in a subsequent chapter.

Chapter Nineteen

What Children Think

A feature which appeared in the *Deseret News* in March of 1977 put into perspective some needs children feel in the home. A survey was taken among elementary school children, the results of which stress the need of honesty and consistency on the part of parents and give an insight into the thinking of these young people.

The *Deseret News* article read:

"Young people want consistent guidance say leaders of 4-H and other extension youth programs at Utah State University. From expressed desires and expectations of fourth grade children the following 13 points of advice to parents and leaders of youth have been derived:

"Don't give me everything I ask for. Sometimes I am just testing you to see how much I can get.

"Don't always be giving orders. If you suggest something instead of giving a command, I will do it later.

"Don't keep changing your mind about what you want me to do. Make up your mind—and stick to it.

"Keep promises. Both good and bad. If you promise a reward, make sure you give it to me. If you promise punishment, make sure I get that, too.

"Don't compare me with anybody else, especially a brother or a sister. If you make me out to be better or smarter, somebody gets hurt. If you make me out to be worse or dumber, then I get hurt.

"Don't correct my mistakes in front of other people. Tell me how to improve when nobody is around.

"Let me do as much for myself as I can. That's how I learn.

"Don't scream at me. It makes me scream back, and I don't want to be a screamer.

"Don't tell lies in front of me or ask me to tell lies to help you out. It makes me think less of you and less of myself, even if I am supposed to be doing you a favor.

"When I do something wrong, don't try to get me to tell you why I did it. Sometimes I don't know why.

"Don't pay too much attention to me when I say I have a stomach ache. Playing sick can be a good way to get out of doing things I don't want to do, or going places I don't want to go.

"When you are wrong about something, admit it. It won't hurt my opinion of you.

"Treat me like you treat your friends. Then I will be your friend and you will be mine."

As is indicated by these replies, children usually reflect the attitudes and habits of their parents, and when youngsters reach the age of those included in that study it is often too late for parents to make sufficient adjustment to correct their own habits.

But if parents will begin to work with their children when they are very small, maintain a proper attitude themselves, and learn to teach gospel principles to the children when they are young, conditions can be entirely different.

In a recent issue of the *Reader's Digest* a very persuasive article urged parents to draw nearer to their little children by telling them bedtime stories. James Daniel, the author, said to parents:

"If you do this even a few minutes a day, the

dividends will be beyond price. You will build a lasting link of shared pleasure and understanding across the generations. . . . It's really a better fortune than any amount of money you could leave your child."

What excellent advice this is! Thousands of Latter-day Saint families have done this over the years and have experienced the rich rewards that result.

Many have not limited their story telling to fairy tales. While all children should know and enjoy the classic fairy tales which have become a part of our literature, fairy tales are not enough. Stories from the scriptures and from Church history can equal the fascination of anything Hans Christian Andersen ever dreamed of—and more.

Parents who tell bedtime stories from the scriptures can teach the gospel to their little ones very effectively by this method and, at the same time, entertain them as well. What better opportunity is there to help children learn to love Joseph Smith, Nephi, Alma, Abinadi, and Moroni, young Samuel in the temple, or the boy Jesus and then the Christ in his adult role? At this impressionable age our little ones may be taught the truths in story form as at few other times in their lives.

The greatest need of our people as a whole is genuine conversion to the gospel, a conversion that will bring lifelong dedication and obedience. Why do some people go astray? Because they are not fully converted. Why is worldliness so attractive to many? Because they have not truly tasted the sweet fruits of the Tree of Life.

Jesus said we must be born again. Our hearts must be touched, our emotions stabilized, our minds instructed, so that we shall stand on solid ground in the face of temptation.

It was no idle word given by the Savior when he commanded us to search the scriptures. Is there any better way to do so than to seek out eternal truths and retell them in story form to our impressionable little ones who ask each evening "Tell me a story"?

Actually it is a way of not only converting our little

ones as we entertain them at bedtime, but also of converting the parents as they make such a custom a part of their family routine.

Parents can also draw close to their children while they educate them in the area of home responsibilities—call them chores if you like. Work is basic in making young people feel a part of the home. This of course includes training in home duties.

For example, a great many girls know little, if anything, about housekeeping. They may have watched their mothers prepare meals, but many young girls have excused themselves from helping, preferring to study their school lessons instead.

But it is this helping which provides the training. Every girl should learn to cook. Every girl should learn to make beds. Every girl should know how to do the family laundry.

Boys should also be taught to work and to love it. They should be encouraged to do chores about the home. This is easy if the family lives on a farm, but even in the city families can arrange to have their boys carry newspapers, work in service stations, assist with janitorial duties, take care of lawns in summer, shovel snow in winter, and many similar things.

Boys and girls who learn to work, and enjoy doing it, seldom get into difficulty. A good work and training program for both boys and girls during their growing-up period can be one of the most valuable things a family can arrange.

Like adults, children need a home base on which they can depend. They need a daily routine of wholesome activities including sleeping, recreation and study. They need to have regular, well-prepared meals. They need to have the loving care of parents who make that home base stable. They need to know the discipline of the home and to know what is right and wrong under the terms of that discipline so that they can work out a well-ordered life.

Young people, with the help of their parents, need to

put their roots down securely in order to stabilize their lives and prepare a foundation of order, of love, of caring, of sharing with others. Only family life can provide this, and without it children will rarely grow up to be the strong citizens they otherwise could become.

Chapter Twenty

Readjusting Our Lives

Inasmuch as the Lord commands that we all perfect ourselves and eventually become even as he is (See Matthew 5:48), it is obvious that he expects us to progress, no matter what our station may be, and to overcome our weaknesses by readjusting our lives.

President McKay used to speak of the gospel as a means of making bad men good and good men better. That is the concept we all should adopt. We can become better if we only will. All can improve.

To assist us in perfecting ourselves, the Lord provided the Church as the means by which we can achieve this improvement. No one alone can reach perfection in any line. All require help from those who are able to give it.

When the Apostle Paul wrote to the Ephesians he explained this principle. He said that the Church is "for the perfecting of the saints, for the work of the ministry, for the edifying of the body of Christ." (Ephesians 4:12.)

But in giving us this definition he also told us the extent to which we are to perfect ourselves. He defined our goal and said we are to achieve "unto a perfect man, unto the measure of the stature of the fulness of Christ." (Ephesians 4:13.)

Christ then is our pattern. Our definition of perfection is that we are to become like him, not in only a few ways but "unto the measure of the stature of the *fulness* of Christ."

The Savior showed us that this is possible, and that this is what is expected. He was Creator of all. He is divine, the Son of Almighty God. But although an infinite and a divine Being, he nevertheless descended below all things when he came to earth. He was born in a stable; cradled in a manger, and wore swaddling clothes as an infant.

When he became an adult, he went to John the Baptist for baptism, just as would any man who believed. In his ministry he walked the plains of Palestine; he hungered at times, and thirsted; he became weary. He was severely criticized and persecuted by his enemies. He was spat upon, maligned, and ignominiously crucified between two thieves.

Why did he descend below all things as he did? It was to show us that no matter how weak we may be we can rise above our own lowly station. Although he descended below all things, he also ascended above all things. He is a perfect demonstration of the fact that no matter what our lot in life may be, we too may arise and eventually reach the measure of the stature of the fulness of Christ. We can become like our Heavenly Father—perfect.

We are his children. We have divinity within us. He opens the door. He provides the means. He holds out to us an urgent invitation:

"Come unto me, all ye that labour and are heavy laden, and I will give you rest. Take my yoke upon you, and learn of me; for I am meek and lowly in heart: and ye shall find rest for your souls. For my yoke is easy, and my burden is light." (Matthew 11:28-30.)

What did he say to the adulterous woman? "Neither do I condemn thee: go, and sin no more." (John 8:11.) What earned this consideration? Repentance.

When the Apostle Peter resisted him, and the Lord

said to Peter "Get thee behind me, Satan: thou art an offence unto me" (Matthew 16:23), and when he denied the Lord thrice just before the crucifixion, what turned Peter into the chief of the apostles? It was repentance.

When Saul of Tarsus turned from a persecutor of the Saints into the great apostle to the gentiles, what accomplished the change? Again, repentance.

And when young Alma and the sons of Mosiah turned from persecutors to missionaries, what brought about the change? It was repentance.

Repentance is open to us all. The whole concept of the gospel is that we lift ourselves above sin and degredation, and rise to Christlike heights. That is why repentance forms such an important part of the gospel. That is why we have remission of sins in baptism. That is why the Lord stressed the importance of forgiveness of sins as he did when he gave us the Lord's prayer. (See Matthew 6:14-15.) That is why, through Ezekiel, the Lord said: "Have I any pleasure at all that the wicked should die? saith the Lord God: and not that he should return from his ways, and live?" (Ezekiel 18:23.)

Jesus died on the cross that all men might come unto him and in doing so receive a remission of sins through baptism. He made it abundantly clear that if we will repent, his suffering on the cross will pay for our sins. (See D&C 19:16-18.) But if we fail to repent, his blood will not cleanse us, and we shall have to pay the price ourselves.

That is what the Prophet Abinadi meant when he said:

"The Lord redeemeth none such that rebel against him and die in their sins; yea, even all those that have perished in their sins ever since the world began, that have wilfully rebelled against God, that have known the commandments of God, and would not keep them; these are they that have no part in the first resurrection. Therefore ought ye not to tremble? For salvation cometh to none such; for the Lord hath redeemed none such; yea, neither can the Lord redeem such, for he cannot deny himself; for he cannot deny justice when it has its claim." (Mosiah 15:26-27.)

That too is why Alma preached that this mortal life is a time of probation that God has allotted us in which to repent from our sins and perfect ourselves and become like him. (See Alma 42:4.)

The further words of Ezekiel are most enlightening on this point. He said:

"If the wicked will turn from all his sins that he hath committed, and keep all my statutes, and do that which is lawful and right, he shall surely live, he shall not die. All his transgressions that he hath committed, they shall not be mentioned unto him: in his righteousness that he hath done he shall live." (Ezekiel 18:21-22.)

But he gives us the other side of the picture too. He says that when a righteous man turns from his righteousness and lives out the rest of his life in sin and dies in his sin, "all his righteousness that he hath done shall not be mentioned: in his trespass that he hath trespassed, and in his sin that he hath sinned, in them shall he die." (Ezekiel 18:24.) This obviously refers to the day of judgment.

The Savior taught a powerful lesson regarding our relationships with other people when he said:

"I tell you this: there is not a thoughtless word that comes from men's lips but they will have to account for it on the day of judgment. For out of your own mouth you will be acquitted; out of your own mouth you will be condemned." (Matthew 12:36, New English Bible version.)

To the Prophet Joseph Smith the Lord said: "He who has repented of his sins, the same is forgiven, and I, the Lord, remember them no more. By this ye may know if a man repenteth of his sins—behold, he will confess them and forsake them." (D&C 58:42-43.)

Forsaking the sin is not enough, as the scriptures indicate. Confession to the proper priesthood authority is likewise necessary, and the Lord has placed the bishops of the wards in their positions as the common judges in Israel for this purpose. And then there is the matter of recompense as far as is within our power.

No joy can come to the wayward person like that

which accompanies true repentance. There is no relief like that of unburdening one's self of sin.

Then, as we take upon us the name of Christ, we will find indeed that his yoke is easy and his burden is light.

Chapter Twenty-one

Homes and Careers

The Church has been a world leader in promoting the welfare, happiness and freedom of women. Mormon women are less circumscribed and are possessed of greater liberty than any women in the world. They received the franchise to vote in 1870, among the first women on earth to be given this right.

LDS women are encouraged to increase their education, widen their outlook upon life, study "out of the best books," and take part in civic affairs. They are encouraged to be active in public elections, to sit in legislatures and help make laws, and to excel in cultural things such as art, music, public speaking, writing and teaching.

They are organized into what is known as the National Women's Relief Society, an organization one million women strong, which promotes the study of literature, history, religion, homemaking, and good citizenry. This organization was effected in 1842 in Nauvoo, Illinois, by the Prophet Joseph Smith. As stated at its inception, the organization was to aid the poor, nurse the sick, and engage in all charitable work as needed, but it is also to elevate womanhood, strengthen the home, and portray exemplary lives in serving the Lord Jesus Christ. As far as our records reveal, the Relief Society was the first women's organization in the world, created for such purposes.

The Church in no way places restrictions upon the advancement of its female members. Rather it advocates and strongly urges their progress in every wholesome respect. But it always preserves the ideal that the highest goal of true womanhood is motherhood, a calling in which a woman can rear children in sound character and in faith in Christ, and help them become good citizens of the land in which they live and proper candidates to come into the presence of the Lord, their Creator.

President Harold B. Lee wrote:

"Woman's influence can bless a community or a nation to that extent to which she develops spiritual powers in harmony with the heavensent gifts which she has been by nature endowed. If she does not forfeit her priceless heritage by her own wilful negligence, she can be largely instrumental in safeguarding democracy and downing a would-be tyrant. Year in and year out she may cast an aura of her calming and refining influence to make certain that her posterity will enjoy the opportunities to develop to their fullest potential of their spiritual and physical nature." (*Relief Society Magazine*, January 1967, page 13.)

Mormon women also have taken a leading part in the development of the rights of women worldwide. Mrs. Belle S. Spafford, president of Relief Society for many years, served as president of the National Council of Women of the United States, and she has served for several years as a U.S. delegate to the World Council of Women. Mrs. Florence S. Jacobsen, former president of the YWMIA, is likewise a U.S. delegate to the World Council of Women, as are also Mrs. Barbara B. Smith, president of the Relief Society of the Church, and Mrs. Ruth Funk, president of the Young Women of the Church. They have served in these capacities with the full endorsement and encouragement of the presiding officers of the Church.

Mormon women have achieved in other areas as

well—in opera and other forms of music, in business and professional careers. But in it all, they have regarded their calling as wives and mothers as paramount. They feel that the highest responsibility God ever gave to women was to rear their children by teaching and directing them in ways of righteousness, thus producing honest citizens of high integrity.

Mrs. Spafford reflected true Mormon ideals when she spoke as follows before the Lochinvar Club in New York City, July 12, 1974:

"Working with women in many countries of the world convinces me that there is no task to which woman may put her hand so broad and inspiring, so filled with interest, so demanding of intelligence and capability, as rewarding as that of wife, mother, and homemaker. I regard this role as taking precedence over all others for women.

"In a well-ordered home, husband and wife approach their responsibilities as a joint endeavor. Together they safeguard the sanctity of the home. Their personal relationship is characterized by respect and enduring love. They cherish their children. In child rearing, I believe, there is no substitute for a caring mother.

"A woman should feel free, however, to go into the market place and into community services on a paid or volunteer basis if she so desires when her home and family circumstances allow her to do so without impairment to her family life.

"Women owe it to themselves to develop their full potential as women—to exercise their mental capabilities, to enlarge upon their talents, and increase their skills, in order that they may give to the world the best they have in a manner that will be productive of the most good, regardless of the paths their lives may take.

"I deplore the far-out views that openly break with those practices and procedures whose tested values over generations of time have contributed to the decency, stability, well-being and happiness of humankind. I accept the premise that moral right is that which is true, ethically good and proper, and in conformity with moral law.

"What was morally right based on truth must remain right regardless of changing times and circumstances. Truth—and right that is based on truth—are immutable. We cannot afford to allow national sensitiveness to become dulled into a calm acceptance of degenerating values and their demoralizing affects on our nation and its people.

"What of tomorrow, I ask?

"May I submit a few opinions, not that I regard myself in the slightest degree as a seer, but merely from the point of view of trends as I observe them and as I draw upon the past as I have noted it.

"Just as the pendulum swings to and fro under the combined action of gravity and momentum to regulate the movements of clockworks and machinery and usually with the first push strikes hard at the far left and far right, moving somewhat irregularly, and then finds its level, thus assuring the proper functioning of the instrument—so I believe will the pendulum of the current women's action program perform.

"Furthermore, I believe that without doubt many of the repressions and injustices which are troubling women today will be resolved. Gratefully, this is already taking place. I cite such things as equal pay for equal work under similar circumstances, new legislation on such things as property rights and non-discrimination credit laws. This portends a better day ahead for woman.

"Borrowing words from Marvin Kalb, 'We have no valid evidence that today's headlines will be tomorrow's wisdom.' Undoubtedly some of the things for which women are clamoring today will be in the discard tomorrow.

"Tomorrow we undoubtedly will hear less of woman's rights and more of her responsibilities and achievements.

"Legislation may make legal the total equality of the sexes, but it is my opinion that the different natures of man and woman will be the supreme law in dictating the divisions of labor to which each will be drawn in the work of the world.

"It is my experience that life, the stern teacher and the great disciplinarian, is now forcing upon us a recognition of the importance of spiritual and moral values. I believe a new day will find us moving forward toward primal religious, spiritual, and moral values, with materialism taking a lesser position. Man cannot live by bread alone.

"I am convinced that the home will stand as it has stood during past generations as the cornerstone of a good society and a happy citizenry. While old activity patterns within the home may be modified by the impact of change outside the home, the enduring values which cannot be measured in terms of their monetary worth, their power for good, the need of the human being for them—such values as peace, security, love, understanding—will not be sacrificed on the altar of new philosophies and new concepts.

"Countless men and women and even children who have tasted these fruits of home and family life will recognize new philosophies which create spoilage in them and they will fend them off. It is in the home that the lasting values of life are best internalized in the individual. It is this which builds good citizens, and good citizens make good nations.

"President Spencer W. Kimball has expressed the belief that the future of the nation, its success and development, are based largely upon the strength of family life. I am confident there are tens of thousands of Americans, men and women, who share this belief.

"Robert O'Brien, senior editor of *Reader's Digest*, in an address given at a woman's conference in New York, had this to say: 'In our hearts, we all know that the home is the cornerstone of American democracy. . . . it's well that the nation recognize and remember it, and engrave it upon the tablets of her history.'

"Throughout the ages children have needed mothers with their love and understanding guidance; men have needed wives, and women have needed husbands to share in the concerns and responsibilities of life. They have needed the happy, loving, and protective companionship of one another. It will ever be so.

"There is an old saying, 'Man must work while woman must wait.' The waiting period for the wheels of progress to roll around in behalf of woman—a period during which woman, herself, has worked as well as waited—is now nearly over. We may now say to her in the words of Solomon, the wise man of Israel, 'Give her of the fruits of her hands; and let her own works praise her in the gates.' (Proverbs 31:31.)"

Chapter Twenty-two

Feminine Fulfillment

 T he opportunities for women to excel are greater today than ever before. We should all be resourceful and ambitious, expanding our interests. Forget self-pity and look for mountains to climb."

So spoke Mrs. Camilla Eyring Kimball as she addressed the second annual Women's Conference at Brigham Young University in February, 1977.

Mrs. Kimball, the accomplished wife of President Spencer W. Kimball, is herself an example of the things she taught the women at Brigham Young University. She has fulfilled a great mission in rearing her family, and yet she has constantly improved her already excellent education, attended special university classes over the years, engaged in cultural, civic, religious and agricultural activities, and allowed herself to reach into even other lines of interest. She was well prepared to address the group and discuss feminine fulfillment.

While asserting the right of women to progress both spiritually and intellectually, as well as in service to the community, Mrs. Kimball sustained the home as the heart string of true progress. She quoted Michael Novak, in *Harper's Magazine*, who said:

"Throughout history, nations have been able to survive a multiplicity of disasters—invasions, famines, earthquakes, epidemics, depressions, but they have never been able to survive the disintegration of the family. The family is the seed bed of economic skills, money habits, attitude toward work, and the art of financial independence. It is a stronger agency of education than the school and stronger for religious training than the church. What strengthens the family strengthens the society. . . . If things go well with the family, life is worth living. When the family falters, life falls apart."

Mrs. Kimball then continued:

"We are in a period when the great propaganda machines are telling us that for a woman to choose a career in home and family is somehow demeaning and that self-respect demands she pursue a profession of law or medicine or business. But rather than directing both marriage partners away from the home, we need to encourage both to make the strengthening of the family their primary concern. There is challenge, accomplishment and satisfaction enough for anyone in this greatest educational endeavor—the home. . . .

"We are by no means the only ones to recognize the importance of the family. Dr. Earl Schaefer at the University of North Carolina has affirmed that 'parents and the home environment are more critical to a child's educational success than schools and teachers are. Three years of research has produced a tremendous amount of evidence that parents' involvement with the child has the greatest impact in achievement, in curiosity, persistence—even creativity.'

"It has long been said that children whose parents have read aloud to them learned to read better and with greater enjoyment than children who did not have such experience. Also, that those coming from homes where books were read, ideas discussed, and art appreciated proved to be better students than those who missed these experiences. . . .

"God joined Adam and Eve in the holy bonds of marriage even before they were mortal and commanded them to cleave to one another; God has through all ages fostered the family. . . .

"My feeling is that each of us has the potential for special accomplishment in some field. The opportunities for women to excel are greater today than ever before. We should all be resourceful and ambitious, expanding our interests. Forget self-pity and look for mountains to climb. Everyone has problems. The challenge is to cope with those problems and get our full measure of joy from life. . . .

"Some of the delightful pleasures of life are in continuing education in our mature years and in the collecting and reading of fine books. Continue to pick up interesting information in history, current events, the arts. There are various areas which we may miss in the few years we are enrolled in college, and learning confined to four years is soon out of date. . . .

"Much unhappiness has been suffered by those people who have never recognized that it is as necessary to make themselves into whole and harmonious personalities as to keep themselves clean, healthy, and financially solvent. Wholeness of the mind and spirit is not a quality conferred by nature or by God. It is like health and knowledge. Man has the capacity to attain it, but to achieve it depends on our own efforts. . . .

"In the Church organization there are ample opportunities for both men and women. I have felt no deprivation in not holding the priesthood. I feel only gratitude that I can with my husband and sons receive all its blessings without my having to assume many of its responsibilities."

Chapter Twenty-three

The Middle Years

Wat does life hold for a woman who has spent some twenty-five years being a full-time mother and homemaker and suddenly finds her "nest" empty?

Will she be able to "cut the cord" and allow her mature children to develop and grow and become independent adults in their own right? Or will she feel the necessity of becoming a "professional mother-in-law" or a grandmother obsessed with the urge to thrust unwanted advice and interference upon the homes of her married children?

I posed these questions to a widely experienced and well-trained adviser in this field. He strongly urged that mothers with little children should look forward to the time when those children are out of school, married, and established in homes of their own.

He gave this advice:

"If the woman has continued to grow, the time she has after the children leave home will provide the opportunity to do all those things she wanted to do when her children were younger. She will be able to build up her relationship with her husband without the interruption of her children's demands, a permanent second honeymoon if she will.

"She may acquire special skills in handicrafts, ethnic cooking, sports, the arts. She may learn to run a computer, earn a college degree, enter the business community, work with the blind, the aged, or the delinquent. She will want to expand her knowledge of her church and reread the scriptures with the added meaning that her maturity provides. And she will want to reexamine her values to insure that she is living a truly Christian life.

"The time for excuses is now over. She no longer says to herself, 'I'll do that as soon as I have the time.' She now has the time and must use it to develop herself. In some cultures women panic when the children leave. Many turn to soap operas, trash novels, and backfence gossip and sometimes become dependent on tranquilizers or alcohol. Others become compulsive eaters and ascribe their calorie-swollen bodies to middle age or going through 'the change.' Some neglect their appearance, their housework, their husbands, their physical well-being, but most important, they neglect their minds.

"The intelligent woman looks to her future in the middle years while she is still very much involved with a young family. She will keep on top of current events as well as reading her scriptures and other books. She knows that the children of readers will become readers themselves.

"She is aware that the most important tool she can give her children in a school situation is enthusiasm for reading. She will reread the children's classics aloud with her own little ones and relish the experience.

"As her children grow, she will read what they read to promote family discussions and gain a feeling for the direction of their interests. She will not allow her mind to be glutted with worthless programs from television any more than she will allow her children's minds to be dominated by the mundane on TV. She will utilize television as an educational experience, not as a baby-tending device.

"The intelligent woman guards her health in her younger years with the same dedication with which she guards the health of her family. She knows that a vibrant feeling of well-being is the result of proper diet and physical activity. A body neglected in the twenties will limit accomplishments in the forties or fifties, so she watches rest and diet and has a complete physical check-up from a trusted medical doctor every year.

"She will not fall into the trap of eating the children's leftovers rather than 'waste' them. She provides smaller portions and discards whatever is left instead of adding it to her waistline. She never lets a day go by without reminding herself that the glory of God is intelligence.

"When dirty floors or soiled diapers might engulf her, she should keep in mind the beautiful and the good and look ahead to the time when she will have opportunity to play a different role in society. She meets her challenges with courage and humor with the certainty that she will never regret time invested in family.

"And when the children are gone, the intelligent woman is not afraid to be alone with herself because she is an interesting and interested person, turned on to the world around her. She sees the horizon beckoning to her, telling her to expand.

"And because she is growing constantly and since growth is a fascinating thing, she will be valued more highly by her husband and children who will constantly discover unsuspected qualities and talents in 'Mom.' The middle years will become a time of discovery, an adventure in reaching upward."

How thrilled newly married couples are just to be in each other's presence! Much of this same thrill may be recaptured when a couple is left alone again after their children have left to make homes of their own. These married couples may achieve a whole new appreciation of each other.

Chapter Twenty-four

The Pioneer Woman

In the days of President Brigham Young, the "gentile" press and its many contributors spoke of Mormon women as mere chattels and slaves of the men of the Church. This of course was but an expression of their total ignorance of the facts, and their oft-repeated prejudices. Mormon women were among the world's leaders in establishing the proper position of women in the world, and their status in many respects was as important as that of the men.

It was a position of course which placed sacred motherhood and homemaking first on the list of priorities, but in which they likewise participated in business affairs, in the arts, in medicine, and in various other enterprises. Even in those pioneer times there was a firm determination to develop the "whole woman," and it had the support and encouragement of the priesthood leaders of the Church.

Mormon women then, as now, took a leading part in the Church organizations, serving as both presidents and counselors in presidencies of the Relief Society, the Young Women, and the Primary Association in all wards, stakes and missions. But they also were storekeepers, printers, telegraphers, silk growers, surgeons and hospital directors. They took part in politics, and were the first women in the world to hold the franchise. They achieved in economic and social activities, enjoying much of the same equality as the men.

In the winter of 1976 the *Brigham Young University Studies* published an illuminating article entitled "Eliza R. Snow and the Woman Question," written by Jill C. Mulvay. With permission I quote a few paragraphs from that discussion.

Sister Mulvay said that with the organization of the Church the women became deeply engaged in helping to establish the kingdom of God on earth. She adds:

"By the 1880s Mormon women had significant duties and responsibilities inside and outside their homes. At the first meeting of the International Council of Women at Washington, D.C. in 1888, Utah's delegate reported that 400 Relief Societies in Utah held property valued at $95,000, many societies owning the halls in which they met. Mormon women published their own biweekly newspaper titled the *Woman's Exponent*. The Relief Society managed a hospital with a woman as resident surgeon. And the women of Zion had contributed significantly to the territory's economy through their participation in silk production and their mercantile cooperatives promoting home manufacture. By the turn of the century Mormon women had made political, economic and social gains within their own culture. . . .

"The focal point of late nineteenth century women's issues was suffrage. In that matter Mormon women were for some years ahead of women involved in the national suffrage movement, women in Utah receiving in 1870 the franchise for which their Eastern sisters would battle for the next five decades. They had staged no demonstrations and apparently circulated no petitions. The signature of Eliza R. Snow headed fourteen signatures on a memorandum to acting territorial governor Stephen Mann praising his 'liberality and gentlemanly kindness' in signing the bill granting suffrage. . . .

"In 1872, while Susan B. Anthony was being arrested in Rochester, New York for her attempt to register and vote, Eliza R. Snow encouraged Mormon women to cast their more easily secured ballots. She possessed enough political acumen to see the advantages of female suffrage, especially in Utah. 'Your vote counts as much, weighs as heavily, as President Young's, Brother G. A. Smith's or Brother D. H. Wells's, hence you should consider yourselves important on election day,' she counseled her sisters. She told Ogden Relief Societies, '(God) has given us the right of franchise,' and it is 'as necessary to vote as to pray.' With Illinois and Missouri persecutions vivid enough in her memory, she advised, 'Unless we maintain our rights we will be driven from place to place. . . .'

"In 1868 the Relief Society was erecting its first hall in the Fifteenth Ward and at the same time Brigham Young was suggesting classes through the University of Deseret 'giving ladies a thorough business education, qualifying them for bookkeepers, accountants, clerks, cashiers, tellers, payers, telegraphic operators, reporters, and other branches of employment suitable to their sex.' Eliza backed him up with the words of her first and best-loved Prophet: 'Joseph Smith counseled the sisters to do business.'

"More than once Eliza Snow helped Brigham Young in his requests for women to meet specific community needs. In 1873 when the President asked women to help with printing, Eliza made up her mind 'to go from house to house if required to procure young ladies to learn.' President Young suggested that young ladies volunteer to study obstetrics and nursing, and to become physicians. 'We want sister physicians that can officiate in any capacity that gentlemen are called upon to officiate. . . . Women can occupy precisely the same footing that men occupy as physicians and surgeons,' declared Eliza. Small groups of women began their own classes in physiology and anatomy, and several women went East to study medicine, some with financial aid from their sisters. By 1879, plans for a hospital were underway, and in 1882, under the direction of Eliza R. Snow, president of its founding association, the Deseret Hospital opened its doors and an LDS woman was installed as resident surgeon. . . .

"In 1876, President Young asked the women to 'form an association to start business in the capacity of disposing homemade articles, such as are manufactured among ourselves.' Eliza Snow was elected president of the Relief Society Woman's Mercantile Association and the women opened their store in the Old Constitution Building on Main Street in Salt Lake City. Because they had no capital to commence their enterprise, they sold on commission and the project came to be known as the Woman's Commission Store. The first year of operation Eliza superintended the store from eight in the morning until six at night, carefully looking after the minute details— evidently quite capably. Once, refusing to let one of Brigham Young's clerks dictate the terms of commission on Young's goods, Eliza haughtily wrote the President: 'Although we are novices in the mercantile business, we are not green enough for that kind of management.' "

Today we honor pioneer women like Eliza R. Snow for their courage and persistence in overcoming the obstacles of a wasteland environment. Side by side with strong men, they conquered a desert and made it blossom—not only with roses, but with hospitals, factories, stores, homes, and with justice, knowledge, and opportunity.

We need pioneer women today to conquer another wasteland—a desert of moral values, a land parched by a famine of hearkening to the word of God. We need women to build strong homes and families, to create beauty and order and personal integrity. Such a woman was Emma Marr Petersen, an accomplished musician who gave much public service through her music, but in addition made a great contribution to the youth and children of the Church through the publication of more than a dozen books of special interest to them.

She developed her talents to give to her associates in the kingdom of God those skills that could meet the needs of present-day living, such as writing, music, compassionate service, leadership and sweet companionship. She assisted in the educational program of the Relief Society which now has expanded into many cultures and which will improve talents and prepare families for the day in which we live.

When Sister Petersen wrote her credo, she said among other things:

"I shall strive always to cultivate and increase my talents for my own self-respect as well as for the good of others.

"I shall always have a project of some kind wherein I shall work to serve others or improve myself intellectually, spiritually or socially.

"To do this I shall fill my mind with thoughts of charity, confidence, contentment and courage.

"I shall entertain no resentment, jealousy, or envy and shall always try to do to others as I would wish to be done by.

"I shall be pleasant, courteous and respectful in dealing with others regardless of their station in life."

Chapter Twenty-five

Hold to Our Moorings

Good families make strong communities, and strong communities make great nations. But the homes built by those families and communities can only be as strong as their allegiance to the Lord Jesus Christ.

It was God who instituted family life. It was he who provided marriage in the first place and commanded that it should be the pattern for mortals through all ages of time.

It is he who commands that we have good family relationships, that we rear children in the faith, that husbands and wives be true to each other, and that charity, love and chastity be prime ideals in our lives.

The Lord has two great avenues for accomplishing his purposes on earth. One is the family, which is the unit designed eventually to lead us to become perfect as he is. The other is his Church by which he implements that process.

The Apostle Paul told the Ephesians that the Church organization headed by apostles and prophets is indeed for the perfecting of the Saints and for their edification, as well as for the work of the ministry. (See Ephesians 4.)

Through the family, bound together by the sealing power of the holy priesthood, we become an eternal unit. Through the Church we learn the principles of perfection. In this sense the program of the Church becomes the instrument of salvation, for it is through activity in that program that we work out our salvation here on earth. Hence we see the great importance of the Church to us. Hence we sense the imperative need that we appreciate the Church and what it has accomplished, as well as what it can and will do for us as individuals if we adhere to its principles.

The Church today is truly a "marvelous work and a wonder." Having started with but six members, it is now approaching the four-million mark, with congregations in approximately seventy countries. Once a persecuted few, it now has become a beacon of light and strength to hosts of people who speak many tongues and who live in the four quarters of the earth.

Being strong as it is, the Church now is able to serve and help its member families more than at any other time, and it holds out an open invitation to all to take part.

Consider for a moment what the Church has done and what it offers. As Latter-day Saints we are committed to sobriety and good character, to honesty and righteous living. We teach virtue and chastity as basic cardinal principles of our faith. We advocate the stability and preservation of the home.

To us the family is the cornerstone of civilization and must ever be. It is the foundation of proper human relationships.

We teach our men and women fidelity in its loftiest meaning. We believe that each of us is a spirit child of God and that the Lord intends that we shall so live that eventually we may become perfect as our Father which is in heaven is perfect. (See Matthew 5:48.)

We believe the family is intended to become an eternal unit, to be projected beyond death and the resurrection into an everlasting and immortal life.

It is to prepare ourselves in worthiness for such a destiny that we teach our high standard of fidelity on the part of both husband and wife. We have but one single standard of morality for all. Our constant cry is "Be ye clean that bear the vessels of the Lord." (D&C 38:42.)

We operate a consistent missionary program. We now have approximately one hundred and fifty proselyting missions with congregations in most of the free world. Ten years ago we had only seventy-four missions. Today we have some twenty-five thousand missionaries, mostly young men about twenty years of age. Ten years ago we had only seven thousand. Ten years ago we had six thousand wards and branches, and now we are approaching ten thousand. Ten years ago we had 412 stakes; now we are nearing 900. They are found in nations from South America to Scandinavia and from Alaska to South Africa to Australia and the islands of the South Seas.

We are generally a healthy people. Dr. James E. Enstrom of the UCLA School of Public Health reported in the *Pasadena Star-News* that the incidence of cancer among the Mormons is 50 percent lower than the national average. In Utah the cancer death rate is the lowest in America.

With respect to lung cancer, LDS women have only 31 percent and men only 38 percent of the national average. For cancer of the esophagus related to alcohol usage, the figure for Latter-day Saints is only 11 percent *of the national average* for women and 34 percent for the men. These figures are provided by Dr. Joseph F. Lyon, director of the Utah Cancer Registry.

The *Statistical Abstract of the United States* for the year 1971 (Bureau of the Census) reported some interesting figures comparing Utah, which is predominantly Mormon, with the rest of the nation. All states in the Union are listed according to frequency of incidence of the diseases mentioned below, with the states placed lowest on the list having the least number of cases.

For diseases of the heart, Utah ranks in forty-sixth place; for influenza and pneumonia, forty-ninth place; for cerebrovascular diseases, forty-sixth place; arteriosclerosis, forty-ninth place; cirrhosis of the liver, forty-fifth place; bronchitis, emphysema, and asthma, thirtieth place; tuberculosis, fiftieth place; venereal diseases, fiftieth place; major cardiovascular and renal diseases combined, fiftieth place; diseases of the cardiovascular system, fiftieth place; vascular lesions affecting the nervous system, fiftieth place; hypertensive heart disease, forty-third place; other hypertensive diseases, fiftieth place; infectious diseases, fiftieth place; complications of pregnancy, forty-sixth place; infant mortality, fiftieth place.

When speaking of these figures for the state of Utah, it should be kept in mind that about 30 percent of the total population do not belong to our Church, but they are included in the Utah state statistics.

Our Church has been a leader in promoting youth development through the Boy Scout program, which Church leaders feel is a very effective organization for the training of boys of all nations, creeds, and peoples.

In the United States as a whole, only 23 percent of the available boys of Scout age are registered as Scouts. But among the Latter-day Saints the percentage is 85.

In the United States, 1.5 percent of the registered Scouts obtain their Eagle award. Among the Latter-day Saints it is 4 percent.

Our Church, as a sponsoring unit for Scouting, ranks second in the United States in the number of sponsoring units. We are exceeded only by the Parent-Teachers Association. In 1974 they sponsored 20,800 units; the Church sponsored 14,344 units. Following our Church came the United Methodist Church with 13,789 and the Roman Catholic Church with 11,734 units.

In this day of juvenile delinquency, we are greatly heartened by the fact that of the 256,000 teenage boys in our Church, 70 percent are actively associated with the Church, and of the 238,000 girls of comparable age, 73 percent are actively associated with the Church. Think of this! A half-million teenage boys and girls devoted to a church which prohibits liquor, tobacco, and premarital sex. Such a group cannot be duplicated anywhere. What a strength this is to families!

Our Sunday School attendance is notable. Fifty-nine percent of all of our little children are in Sunday School every Sunday, and of the teenage group, every Sunday 60 percent of all LDS youth are present in their classes.

In our Church we teach that "the glory of God is intelligence." (See D&C 93:36.) We believe also that the glory of man is likewise intelligence. With this in mind, we are strong advocates of education.

When Dr. Clark Kerr, chairman of the Carnegie Council on Policy Studies in Higher Education, addressed the commencement exercises of the University of Utah, he made these interesting statements:

"Utah stands first in the nation in the total population ages 3 to 34 enrolled in school.

"Utah stands first in the percentage of the total population enrolled in school at every age level except ages 16-17, where Minnesota ranks first. . . .

"Utah stands first in the average years of school completed for all of its citizens age 25 and older. . . .

"Utah stands first in expenditures on the operating programs of medical schools per $100,000 of personal income in the state."

And then he said: "The Carnegie Commission on Higher Education surveyed the performance of higher education in each of the 50 states. It found Utah, unlike many states, to have no major deficiencies."

Then he asked: "Why has Utah done so well? It is neither the richest, nor the oldest, nor the best located state for educational development. If one could find its secret, perhaps it could be exported elsewhere. But this is not easy, for its secret, I think, is its history. Your early leaders placed a great emphasis on education." And he then quoted Brigham Young in his advocacy of education.

This educational background is reflected in the number

of our people who have reached places of prominence in the United States, Canada, and the world.

Latter-day Saints have filled cabinet positions in the United States and other important positions in Canada. We have our generals and admirals in the military forces. Our people have served regularly in the U.S. Congress over the years, as well as in governing bodies in Canada.

Latter-day Saints have served likewise in important positions on the Federal Reserve Board, the U.S. Customs Court, U.S. Tariff Commission, and in Federal Housing Administration positions.

Dr. Harvey Fletcher, a Mormon high priest, developed stereophonic sound; another Mormon, Philo Farnsworth, was a leading developer of television.

Mormon men have been world presidents of Rotary International and Lions International. They have headed the American Medical Association, the American Bankers Association, and various scientific societies. Also they have held many other positions of importance in scientific research, business, and finance, too many to mention here.

Mormon women are possessed of greater liberty than any women in the world. They understand the true meaning of liberty and justice for all, because it is part of their religion and is fundamental in their daily routine.

There is no worldly bastion equal to our Church for the defense and preservation of the family. In the interest of its own success, every family therefore should make the Church the center of its activity.

As a means of rearing children successfully, every family should bring the gospel into its everyday living. As the gospel saves individuals, it also saves families and holds them together.

It is the Church which provides the eternal marriage bond without which we cannot become "perfect as your Father which is in heaven is perfect." Its priesthood imparts the sealing power that binds family groups into an eternal unit.

With the Church, marriage is forever, families are forever, and individuals find their highest expression within its fold. Man's ways are not God's ways, but God's ways, straight and narrow though they be, lead to life and joy everlasting. Sad it is that so "few there be that find it."

Index

honor in, 67
successful, 11
well-ordered, 93
work responsibilities for children
at, 84
worldly attack on, 21
Home base, importance of, 84
Home evening, 66
Honesty, 18
Honor, 67
Housecleaning, 102

-I-

Ideals, Mormon, 93-95
Illness, 82
Impurity, sexual, 16
India, population problem in, 46
Indulgence, 71
Influences, worldly, 70

-J-

Jacobsen, Florence S., 92
Jesus Christ, 83, 87, 88, 89
gospel of, 4
Jews, 25
Judging, 37
Judgment, day of, 89

-K-

Kimball, Camilla Eyring, 97
on home and family, 98-99
on opportunities for women, 98-99
Kimball, Spencer W., on bearing
children, 23
on eternal marriage, 23-24, 30
on juvenile delinquency, 61
on love and marriage, 35-36
on marriage within one's faith, 12
on nation's future, 95
on preservation of home, 33
on working wives, 61

-L-

Latter-day Saints, in places of
prominence, 113

Lee, Harold B., on being single, 56
on preparation for eternal marriage,
16-17
on standards of right and wrong, 80
on woman's influence, 92
Liberation, 58, 59
Life, family, 5
purpose of, 6
Living, formula for, 37
gospel, 3-4, 86, 113
righteous, 5
Love, 22, 35-36, 77-78
commandment to, 36-37
"Love at Home," 33-34
Lying, 82

-M-

Man, teachings of, 9
uprightness of, 5
Marriage, 35, 108, 113. *See also*
Eternal Marriage
Church view of, 20
civil, 14, 30
for the wrong reasons, 55
happiness in, 21, 36
love in, 78
open, 50
ordained of God, 6
outside of Church, 17
partnership in, 65, 66, 67
purpose of, 22, 44,
sacredness of, 20
sacred relationship, 16
sacrifice in, 36
sex in, 23
success in, 18, 65
teenage, 68
to unbelievers, 11
unselfishness in, 36
use of, as theme in scriptures, 39-40
within one's faith, 12, 14, 18
within the Church, 13, 14
McKay, David O., on chastity, 79
on children, 67
on curtailing birth of children, 43
on father's responsibility to family,
65
on gospel living, 4, 86

-S-

Sacrament, 25, 26
Salvation, 109
Satan, father of contention, 19
    influence of, 17
Screaming, 82
Scriptures, stories from, 83
Sealing, keys of, 28
Sex, desire for, purpose of, 23
Sill, Sterling W., on uprightness of
    man, 5
Sins, forgiveness of, 88-89
Sin, sexual, 79-80
Single state, advice on, 16, 55-56
    crime and, 57
"Singles," 51-52
Smith, Barbara B., 92
Smith, George Albert, on gospel
    living, 3
Smith, Joseph, on calling of Elijah, 28
    on eternal increase, 8
    on gospel ordinances, 26
    on the endowment, 29
    on importance of sealing ordinances,
        28-29
Smith, Joseph F., on curtailing birth of
    children, 43-44
    on home, 34-35
    on sexual sin, 79
Smith, Joseph Fielding, on creation of
    man, 7
Snow, Eliza R., 104-105, 106
    on heavenly parentage, 7
    on voting, 105
    on women as physicians, 106
Socialism, and hunger, 48
Spafford, Belle S., 92
    on Mormon ideals, 93-95
Standards, 80
Statistics, cancer among Mormons,
    110-111
    Church population, 16
    conversion of non-member spouses,
        17
    juvenile delinquency, 60
    marriage outside of the Church, 17
    missionaries, 110
    population in Australia, 46

Sunday School attendance, 112
    teenage Church activity, 111-112
    teenage marriage, 68
    unmarried American couples, 51-52
    U.S. birthrate, 42
    U.S population, 42
Stories, bedtime, 82-84
Success, educational, of children, 98
Suffrage, Mormon women and, 104

-T-

Tanner, N. Eldon, on gospel living, 4
Teachings, man-made, 9
Television, as educational experience,
    101-102
    effects on family, 72-75
    hours spent viewing, 74
    impact on children, 73
    parental guidance in viewing, 76
    sponsors, 74, 75
    violence, 74-75
Temple, Nauvoo, 29
    Salt Lake, 29
    veil, 30-31
    worthiness to enter, 15
Temples, celestial room, 30, 31
    importance of, 29-30
    purpose of, 26, 27, 29, 31
    sealing rooms, 30
Ten Commandments, warning
    contained in, 16
Ten Virgins, parable of, 38-39
    significance of, 39
Terrestrial glory, 14, 18
Time, budgeting, responsibility of
    fathers in, 66
    quality of, devoted to family, 70
Training, of youth, 78
    value of, 78
Truth, 94

-U-

Unbelievers, marriage to, 11
Unchastity, 79
Unhappiness, 99
United States, birthrate, 42
    population, 47